HOW TO BECOME A
WEALTHY
REAL ESTATE
INVESTOR

101 Things You Need to
Know Right Now

TAI A. DESA

Copyright © 2023 Tai A. DeSa
All rights reserved.
No part of this publication may be reproduced, distributed or transmitted in any form or by any means, including photocopying, recording or other electronic or mechanical methods, without the prior written permission of the publisher, except in the case of brief quotations, reviews and other noncommercial uses permitted by copyright law.

Dedication

This book is dedicated to all the people who work to build wealth through real estate. You seek knowledge, build relationships, take risks, invest money, and work long hours to build a brighter future. For those of you who are committed to taking your wealth to the next level, I wrote this book for you.

To Amira. Thank you for loving me when I had no money. Look where we are now, and dream of what we can build from here.

To Alexis and Ashley. You are my greatest achievements. I look at you at five and see your beauty and innocence shining through.

To my past partners, teammates, employers, and advisors, in every season of my life. The good days and the bad days all turned out to be what I needed to be a better investor and a better man.

CONTENTS

Introduction: Why You Should Read This Book xi

1. Spend at Least 10 Minutes a Day Looking for a Deal.....1
2. Forge at Least One New Relationship a Week..........3
3. Money Chases Deals, So Be a Skilled Dealmaker........6
4. Know the Difference Between Growing Cash and Growing Wealth...............................10
5. Tired Landlord = Great Deal......................13
6. Don't Buy Properties Sight Unseen..................16
7. Read These Books..............................18
8. Buy a 2-4 Family Property Using a VA, FHA, or Conventional Loan.............................20
9. Not All Foreclosures Are Deals....................22
10. Find the Deals Hiding in Plain Sight on the Multiple Listing Service................................24
11. Do a Slow Flip on Your Own Residence..............26
12. Buy the Loser in the Neighborhood..................28
13. Don't Go Over Budget..........................29
14. Buy Back Your Time...........................33

15. Know the After Repair Value Before You Make an Offer............................35
16. Take Time to Develop Your Business Strategy..........38
17. Don't Change Course Mid-Stream...................41
18. Buy Close to Home...............................43
19. Create a Free Sales Force........................45
20. Don't Use All Your Credit on a Deal, Especially if Your Business Partner is Not Using Theirs.............47
21. Don't Add Unnecessary Partners....................49
22. You Get What You Tolerate........................51
23. Do Not Partner with a Contractor Who Says They'll Do the Renovation Work...........53
24. How to Evaluate a Contractor Before Hiring Them.....55
25. Start Your Renovation Project the Moment You Buy the Property................................57
26. Create So Much Value for Your Contractors That They Put Your Needs First........................59
27. Don't Fight City Hall............................61
28. Don't Cut Corners on Renovations, and Don't Over-Improve Properties Either................63
29. Change the Locks................................65
30. Deal with the Roof First........................67
31. Complete Your Renovation Project Before Jumping to the Next One..........................69
32. Get It in Writing...............................71
33. Walk the Job Site at Least Twice a Week.............73

34. Convert a 4/1 Into a 3/2.........................75
35. When Flipping an Entry-Level House,
    Wait 90 Days Before Putting It on the Market.........77
36. Know Your True Financial Picture....................79
37. If Your Credit Score is Not Where It Needs to Be,
    Get It There as Fast as Possible......................81
38. Know and Use the Legitimate Tax Deductions and
    Exemptions..84
39. File Your Taxes on Time.............................87
40. Don't Create Too Many Entities.....................89
41. Pay for Legal Insurance............................91
42. Don't Sign Up for Too Many Subscription Services,
    or the Monthly Fees Will Eat You Alive..............93
43. Keep Your Expenses Low and Get Them Lower.........95
44. Go to Seminars, Yet Don't Spend Thousands of
    Dollars on Materials in the Hype of the Moment......97
45. Questions Are the Answer...........................99
46. Constantly Improve Your Negotiation Skills..........101
47. The Purpose of Negotiation is for the Parties to
    Be Satisfied.......................................103
48. Never Give a Concession Without Getting a
    Concession..105
49. Don't Put Too Many Weasel Clauses into
    Your Contract.....................................107
50. Make Lots of Offers and Go for No.................109

51. Become Masterful in Negotiating Over Terms and
    Not Just the Price................................111
52. Serve the Underserved Markets and
    Make More Money..................................113
53. Always Ask for the Best Price....................115
54. Understand and Evaluate Risk.....................116
55. When in Doubt, Hire a Professional...............119
56. Always Have More Than One Vendor.................120
57. Don't Allow Cognitive Shortcuts to Ruin Your
    Decision-Making Ability..........................122
58. Do Your Due Diligence or Pay the Price Later.....124
59. Get to the Potential Deal Faster Than Anyone Else.....126
60. Be Willing to Walk Away..........................128
61. "No" Is a Complete Sentence......................129
62. The Asking Price Is Irrelevant to an Investor....130
63. If a Tenant Is Not Paying Their Rent, Take Action.....131
64. Increase Your Rate of Learning by
    Making More Mistakes.............................133
65. Create Systems...................................135
66. The #1 Skill for Success in Today's
    World is to Be Indistractable....................136
67. Think for One Hour Every Day.....................138
68. When You Know What Market Cycle You Are in,
    It's Time to Prepare for the Next Market.........140
69. Low Price Does Not Always Mean a High Profit.....142
70. Treat Your Family as Your #1 Client..............144

71. Build a Board of Directors for Your Business..........146
72. Don't Skimp on Safety..........................148
73. Scale Your Business............................150
74. Be Proficient in These Four Areas...................155
75. Be Willing to Pay a Premium to Buy the
    House Next Door...............................157
76. Know Your Big Why.............................159
77. Build a Moat Around Your Assets..................161
78. Make One More Call............................163
79. Keep a Journal................................164
80. Own What You Can Rent to Others One Day.........165
81. Give, with Purpose.............................167
82. People Show You Who They Are. Believe Them......168
83. One Dollar of Passive Income Is
    Worth 10 Dollars of Active Income.................169
84. Invest Every Dollar of Passive Income
    Into Another Asset That Produces Passive Income.....171
85. Create Multiple Income Streams...................173
86. Ensure That You Have Signed Leases...............175
87. Don't Cannibalize One Unit to Fix Another Unit......177
88. Never Go More Than Three Straight Years
    Without Increasing the Rent......................178
89. Give Your Spouse or Business Partner Veto Power.....180
90. If Your Spouse or Partner is Completely Against
    Owning Investment Real Estate, Invest in REITs......182
91. Add Something New Every Year....................184

92. Lowest Price Does Not Equal Lowest Cost.. 185
93. Put Your Focus More on Being Effective Than on Being Efficient. 187
94. Have at Least Six Months of Working Capital. 188
95. The Three Questions to Ask When Hiring Someone.. . . .190
96. In the Long Run, the Constraint on Your Business is Your Ambition. 192
97. Find Ways to Make Real Estate Investing Fun. 194
98. Fix the Problem, Not the Blame.. 196
99. Focus on Getting Rich for Sure Instead of Getting Rich Quick. 198
100. Build Wealth That Will Outlast You. 200
101. Be a Victor, Not a Victim.. 202

Epilogue. 205
About the Author. 207
Acknowledgments 209

INTRODUCTION

WHY YOU SHOULD READ THIS BOOK

You were meant for more. If you purchased this book, you want more out of life. If someone gave you this book, they know you are capable of great things and want to see you achieve them.

The ideas in this book are blunt, to the point, easy to understand, and easy to do. Many investors have real estate investing books that they don't read. This book was written so you would actually read it instead of having it collect dust somewhere.

Whether you are a wholesaler, flipper, landlord, developer, agent, property manager, auctioneer, or brand new to it all, this book will help you save money, avoid mistakes, increase profit margins, and skillfully use your talent. Much of the advice here is stated as a rule or commandment. The ideas are based on real-world situations, past experiences, and, frankly, what works.

The nuggets in this book will help you ask better questions and discover better answers on your path to greater wealth.

Real estate investing is not a zero-sum game. Other people don't have to lose when you win. When you succeed more and more, you grow personally, support your family, help the families of the people you hire, and impact the community. Your legacy grows.

Costly mistakes have been my greatest teacher. You don't have to pay the high price I did, so let my past mistakes guide you. Although the content of the book is designed to help you make money in real estate, the recommendations are typically applicable to other businesses. Don't invest another dollar until you've read this book.

To go into more detail on a variety of real estate topics, go to my website at **https://investandtransform.com/**

1

SPEND AT LEAST 10 MINUTES A DAY LOOKING FOR A DEAL.

Even if you have no money to invest right now, invest at least 10 minutes a day looking for a potential deal. Why? Another investor might want the deal you discover, and you could earn an assignment fee for it. Maybe they will want to partner with you. In real estate partnerships, you could be an equal partner by bringing know-how, grit, confidence, and sweat equity to the table, whereas your partner could supply the money.

By searching for at least 10 minutes a day, you will improve your analytical skills to recognize deals even faster in the future. Speed gives you an edge. You will develop a valuable intuition. You will learn more about neighborhoods, property values, and the dollar per square foot that the best properties command. When a house is selling for less than the typical dollar per square foot in the area, you'll know it right away.

HOW TO BECOME A WEALTHY REAL ESTATE INVESTOR

Consistently take a drive or, better yet, go jogging in your target neighborhood. You might as well improve your health while you increase your wealth. When you see a For Sale sign, dial the number to find out more. Opportunity awaits on the other side of the phone call. Look for neglected houses.

Searching online every day will make you sharp. Look for your county's posting of the upcoming foreclosure auctions. Type "sheriff's sale in _____ county" or "foreclosure auction in _____ county" in your Internet search engine. Follow the websites of local real estate auctioneers. Go to your county tax assessor's website to find out how to view the public records for properties in your target neighborhood. Knowing what the owner paid, the property taxes, the assessed value, and the square footage gives insight into what price a potential seller might accept. Ask a Realtor to connect you to a Multiple Listing Service (MLS) portal or to set you up on an automated email list.

Searching daily will give you clues into which real estate agents specialize in investor properties. When you develop a relationship with an investor-friendly agent, you don't just get them—you gain access to their whole network of contractors, lenders, inspectors, investors, and appraisers. Perhaps they will even know an investor who wants to purchase the deals you discover. Maybe that agent knows a tired landlord or motivated seller looking to offload a burdensome house.

Search for potential deals first thing in the morning when it is quiet and before the busyness of the day overtakes you. Some properties may be listed online late at night, and you'll be the first one to lay eyes on them early in the morning.

The more deals you discover, the more money you will make.

2

FORGE AT LEAST ONE NEW RELATIONSHIP A WEEK.

Your network is your net worth. Develop at least one new connection every single week. It could be to a handyman, a general contractor, a plumber, an electrician, or a painter. It could be a real estate agent, a landlord, a surveyor, an appraiser, a house flipper, or a wholesaler.

After serving overseas in the Navy for five straight years, I moved back to the U.S. to become a full-time real estate investor. I didn't know anyone in the real estate, banking, or contracting industries. I started my network by going to the secretary at the church I attended as a youth. I asked her if she knew a real estate agent. She did. I said, "Could you call that agent and tell him about me?" She called the agent and told him to expect my call. I then called the agent and said, "I am building a growing real estate investment business, and I have a lot of business to give to a real estate agent. I'd like to meet with you for 15 to 20 minutes over coffee so I can find out more about you and your business. Can you meet with me on Tuesday at 1:00 p.m. or on Wednesday at 10:00 a.m.?" The agent was excited to meet with me. In the meeting, I asked him about his goals and what kinds of referrals he needed to grow his business. He appreciated that I was curious about how to help him. Then he asked me how he could help me with my business. I replied, "As you know, I am building a growing real estate investment business, and I have a lot of business to give to a plumber. Who do you know that is a plumber?" The agent told me about a plumber he knew well. I asked, "Could you call that plumber and tell him about me?" The agent called the plumber right away. When I dialed the plumber, he immediately took my call. When I met with the plumber, I asked for a referral to an electrician. When I met with the electrician, I asked for a referral to a landscaper. I build a wide and deep network one coffee shop meeting at a time.

Tell people that you are searching for an investment property. Ask people, "Who do you know that I should know?" Tell them that you are looking for a motivated seller. A motivated seller is someone who might need to sell quickly or is someone who has problems with their property. Ask people to think of you first when they come across a fixer-upper. Ask them to contact you right away when they hear someone talking about selling their house or complaining about their property. For example, if someone you know hears a frustrated landlord talk about tenants who are not paying rent, then that landlord is a potential seller you should meet.

When many people know you are looking for an investment property, they may contact you when they come across a potential deal. Sometimes the referrals they make are to a property that is not yet for sale and that no one else knows about. You could be the only game in town to a motivated seller.

When you know a lot of people who likewise know you are looking for an investment property, that's like having a free sales force. A company owner would have to pay thousands of dollars for an in-house sales team, whereas, through consistent networking, you can have leads sent your way *for free*.

When you know more contractors, you'll be able to negotiate the best pricing and the best work completion timeline. Finding great contractors can take some effort, yet it will be well worth it. The best way to find contractors is by asking your friends and family who they know. If someone has hired a contractor and experienced excellent results, then that's a contractor you need to meet. I knew a home inspector who also sang in a rock band. I told him I needed a referral to a remodeling contractor. He told me about a person who likewise sings in a band and is a general contractor. After being connected with that person I asked him to provide an estimate for a house I was under contract to buy. I was impressed with what he said, and I hired him. I liked how he worked. I would hire him again.

Great contractors will give you insights on how to keep renovation costs under control. When I asked one plumber to install a new bathtub and shower surround—a $2,500 multi-day job—he suggested I consider refinishing the tub and shower with epoxy. My wife found a tub refinishing specialist who made the tub look as good as new in only four hours, at a total cost of only $450. Our plumber saved us $2,050, and out of gratitude, we still refer business to him today.

3

MONEY CHASES DEALS, SO BE A SKILLED DEALMAKER.

Yes, you need money to do deals. It can be someone else's money. If you are influential, real estate deals can be pulled off with none of your own money.

Money chases deals. If you are under contract with a screaming hot deal, people with money will be interested under two conditions:

You must demonstrate that there is value in the property, and

You must demonstrate that there is value in working with you.

Private investors look just as hard for skilled, trustworthy dealmakers as they do for lucrative deals. Be the type of person who wealthy people want to be around. Show up on time for meetings. Be prepared. Study the market. Cite statistics. Dress well. Speak well. Be genuine. Smile often.

There are investors willing to put up 100 percent of the money if they believe in you and like the deal you negotiated. There are investors willing to buy a deal from you. There are investors who will lend you money. There are investors willing to connect you with other movers and shakers.

Many years ago when I didn't have a lot of money, I placed a $25 ad in a local Homeowners' Association newsletter. The ad simply stated, "We buy houses cash. Any property, any condition. Quick offer, quick closing." A man who owned a recently vacated rental house called and asked me to look at his property. He said he wanted it sold in two weeks. I told him that to make it happen that fast, the price would have to be well below fair market value. I asked, "What will you take?" He said he wanted $90,000. I knew that was an attractive price. I created an assignable sales contract to buy it for $90,000.

I went to a weekly networking group I had co-founded, and I asked for a connection to a cash investor who wanted a hot deal. The residential mortgage broker in the group said he had just played golf with a house flipper who complained that it was so hard to find houses. The mortgage broker immediately connected me with the flipper. I also went to the title agent in the networking group and asked him to plan for a closing in less than two weeks.

A couple of days later, the flipper went to the house with me and looked at it for a mere 10 minutes. I told him that I was under contract to buy it for $90,000. I said I wanted a $15,000 fee to assign the contract, and I added that he had to close in 11 days. I said that my preferred title company had already conducted a title search and was preparing for the closing. The flipper stepped outside on the front porch, lit a cigarette, and said "I'll take it." He wrote a check to me for $7,500 right there. At the closing 11 days later, he wrote a second check to me for $7,500. He purchased the house for $90,000. The flipper removed the junk, painted the interior, cleaned the home, and sold it a few weeks later for $150,000. He ended up buying five more of my deals, making me over $100,000 in profit.

The owner of a heating oil company saw my website and asked to meet. He said he had a lot of cash and wanted to flip houses. He said he was too busy to find and manage deals. He said he'd be willing to provide all the cash if my team found the deal, negotiated it, managed the renovation, and sold it. The oil company owner said we could split the profit 50-50. We created a joint venture in which both his Limited Liability Company (LLC) and my LLC were on the deed.

Through direct mail to people facing foreclosure, I found a fixer-upper in which the owner still had equity. As proof of funds, I showed the seller a printout of the oil company owner's bank statement. Our joint venture purchased the property. I obtained contractor estimates and selected the best one. I went to the house every other day to observe progress. I gave my joint venture partner an email update and a phone call every week. When the renovation was completed, I hired a Realtor to sell the house. The oil company owner was made whole first, and then we split the profit evenly.

That first deal built trust between us. We had great rapport and established a business rhythm through my way of updating him. We did more deals together. In some cases, he trusted me enough to let me buy houses without him seeing them first.

The co-owner of a real estate brokerage I joined observed me doing business over a couple of years. He then approached me and said that he had $160,000 in a self-directed IRA that he wanted to lend. He said he was too busy to go look at houses, and he just wanted an experienced and trustworthy person to make him a profit. He said that I had to pay him $170,000 in six months or less. Using that money, I bought a short sale townhouse for $127,000. Five years earlier, that newly-built townhouse had sold for $299,900. I spent $15,000 on renovations to include fresh paint, installation of granite countertops, and carpet stretching. I hired a home stager for $1,000 and spent $2,500 on rental furniture. I hired a fellow Realtor from the brokerage to list the townhouse. We obtained multiple offers and sold it for $203,000. The investor made his $10,000 profit and received his $160,000 principal back in five months. I made $35,000 using none of my own money.

The money is out there. To get it, you need to put yourself out there.

4

KNOW THE DIFFERENCE BETWEEN GROWING CASH AND GROWING WEALTH.

Wholesaling and flipping houses, when done well, generate cash. Owning real estate for the long-term creates massive wealth. Begin with the end in mind: Why are you investing in real estate?

If you're good at wholesaling or flipping, you'll be selling each of your properties in less than a year. That means your profit will be a short-term capital gain, equivalent to your ordinary income tax rate. The better you are at cranking out deals, the higher your tax bracket. If you're in the 24 percent tax bracket, that means up to 24 percent of your hard-earned money is going to Uncle Sam.

The ultra-wealthy keep assets for the long-term. If they're in real estate, and many of them are, they are buying and then leasing their properties to others. Essentially, rental income is not taxed as much as flip income because rental income is offset by depreciation, operating expenses, and mortgage interest. Your tenants help you pay down your loan while all the buyers and sellers in the area drive up your property value over time. Your accountant helps you save on taxes by depreciating the asset on your tax returns.

Wholesaling and flipping create active income. You need to keep doing the work. You're only as good as your last deal. Holding and renting real estate creates passive income. As a landlord, you have less work to do. If you hire a professional property manager or have other systems in place, you may have no work to do except talk to your team occasionally.

In my first seven years in real estate, I wholesaled or flipped over 200 properties. My biggest regret is that I only kept one property for myself. I had cash coming in and out, but at the end of those seven years, I didn't create lasting wealth. I failed to create passive income. I failed to create long-term equity. I failed to leverage all those tax deductions.

There is nothing wrong with wholesaling or flipping. There are TV shows galore about house flipping. It's fast, fun, and sexy. Getting a big check at closing is worthy of a big celebration.

Buying and holding are neither fast nor sexy. There aren't any TV shows about landlords that I can find. It's slow and steady, like the tortoise in the fable of the tortoise and the hare. We all know who wins that race.

Many cash-strapped new investors have told me that they will start as a wholesaler, eventually graduate to a flipper when they have enough cash, and then one day in the indeterminate future graduate again to being a landlord. Yet wealth building does not have to follow that sequence. You can start as a landlord right away. More on that later in this book.

Flip if you want. Sell the asset if you can use the cash for something better. If you're serious about building wealth, hang on to most of your assets.

5

TIRED LANDLORD = GREAT DEAL.

When you find tired landlords, you can find solid real estate deals. I'm not talking about sleepy landlords. I'm talking about a rental owner who is sick and tired of dealing with toilets, tenants, and termites. A tired landlord is frustrated and ready to sell, even if they have not thought much about selling.

The tired landlord could be any age. In many instances, it could be someone in their late 60s or older. They've owned their rental properties for decades and might not have any debt. They're tired of personally managing their properties, and there is probably some deferred maintenance. They want to enjoy retirement, whether traveling the world or bouncing a grandkid on their knee. They might even relish the opportunity to mentor or loan money to a young and hungry investor.

Another type of tired landlord could be an accidental landlord. They had to relocate suddenly for their job, and they opted to rent their house from a distance. Unskilled as a landlord and living too far away to keep an eye on the property, they're tired of complaints from the tenant, the neighbors, and the city. Other accidental landlords include the heirs of the deceased.

Yet another type of tired landlord is one who allows tenants to get away with things like late rent payments or non-payments, allows adults not on the lease to move in, permits damage from the tenants, and allows unauthorized pets. The landlord knows they need to enforce breaches of the lease, yet they don't have the stomach or the skills to do so. They just want out.

One more tired landlord is the one who is too old or too busy to personally maintain the property. They know it needs a lot of repairs, which they used to do themselves. Since they don't want to pay for a contractor or they can't afford one, they neglect the property more and more. Other times, vacancies increase, delinquencies increase, and costs go up.

Many landlords don't want their tenants to be fully aware that the building may be for sale. Others may be reluctant to allow many showings. Some landlords may balk at a Realtor's commission. Therefore, these owners may welcome a private sale.

Some tired landlords may be willing to provide owner financing. Many may have little to no debt remaining on the property. Some landlords may appreciate earning interest on a loan or a future share of the profit if the property is rented or sold. Many may wish to defer or minimize their capital gains taxes.

If you have skill (or at least no fear) in dealing with problem tenants and problem properties, you could become a tired landlord's saving grace. Once you acquire a property, you could resolve the tenant's problems or find a way to move them out. If the property needs work, you could increase the value by fixing it up. Your ability to solve problems will make you a pleasant alternative to a tired landlord's stressors. When someone is emotionally fed up with a property, they might be willing to let it go for a low price.

How do you find tired landlords? They are in investor groups. Realtors, bankers, accountants, and lawyers know them. Perhaps you can tell people in your sphere of influence that you're looking for a landlord who frequently complains. A great way to track down tired landlords is to call For Rent signs and strike up a conversation. Tell them that you're a real estate investor who wants to be the first person they call when they are ready to talk about selling.

By making many calls, over time, you'll receive many calls. When you do, ask lots of questions about the property and the situation. If you think you need it, ask the person if they would like to earn additional money on top of the sale price. If they say yes, you have an open door to discuss owner financing options. Regardless, ask the tired landlord what they would need to walk away from the property. They just might name you a price that you can't turn down.

6

DON'T BUY PROPERTIES SIGHT UNSEEN.

If you cannot get into a property to see it, touch it, and get a feel for it, don't bother buying it. More foreclosures these days are being listed by banks on auction websites like auction.com or hubzu.com, and many times the former occupant is still in the house. Therefore, buyers cannot enter the premises to see the house themselves. Your risk increases exponentially when you (and your home inspector or contractor) cannot gain access to the property.

I knew a house flipper who borrowed money from a private lender for a six-month term. The flipper used the cash to purchase an occupied house sight unseen at the county foreclosure auction. The flipper assumed that the owner would leave and that the house would be renovated and sold in less than six months. However, the former owner of the house hired an attorney and refused to move out. It took 13 months of legal action before the former owner could be forced out. When that finally happened, a contractor started working on the renovation. The contractor discovered significant moisture and mold in the lower level. The day the contractor discovered it, the private lender happened to stop by the house. The contractor did not know that the man who stopped by was the lender, and he told him all about the mold issues. The lender decided that this was the last time he would loan money to this flipper.

Even though it may seem like such a property could sell at a significant discount to fair market value, the unknowns could prove more costly. There are plenty of other lucrative properties where you can have a showing, bring in a contractor, and even have a home inspection contingency. Don't jeopardize your financial standing by taking a huge risk.

The very first property I bought was a 5-unit apartment building in inner-city Philadelphia. I bought it sight unseen at an auction. Only one of the five tenants paid rent to me. The ancient heating system did not work. The natural gas line leaked, and the gas company shut it off on a Friday night so the tenants had no hot water. Raw sewage backed up into the basement, and I had trouble finding a plumber who would fix the problem. A contractor took money from me and failed to complete the work. Six weeks after I purchased the building, one of the tenants killed another one of the tenants. While I learned valuable lessons from this property, the most important lesson was to purchase only what I could first see inside and out.

7
READ THESE BOOKS.

Rich Dad, Poor Dad: What the Rich Teach Their Kids About Money—That the Poor and Middle Class Do Not! By Robert T. Kiyosaki with Sharon L. Lechter

The Millionaire Real Estate Investor by Gary Keller with Dave Jenks and Jay Papasan

MONEY Master the Game: 7 Simple Steps to Financial Freedom by Tony Robbins

Getting More: How You Can Negotiate to Succeed in Work and Life by Stuart Diamond

Hold: How to Find, Buy, and Rent Houses for Wealth by Steve Chader, Jennice Doty, Jim McKissack, and Linda McKissack with Jay Papasan

Flip: How to Find, Fix, and Sell Houses for Profit by Rick Villani and Clay Davis

Think and Grow Rich by Napoleon Hill

The Millionaire Next Door: The Surprising Secrets of America's Wealthy by Thomas J. Stanley and William D. Danko

Cashflow Quadrant: Rich Dad's Guide to Financial Freedom by Robert T. Kiyosaki with Sharon L. Lechter

The 4-Hour Workweek: Escape 9-5, Live Anywhere, and Join the New Rich by Tim Ferriss

Unshakeable: Your Financial Freedom Playbook by Tony Robbins with Peter Mallouk

Buy, Rehab, Rent, Refinance, Repeat: The BRRRR Rental Property Investment Strategy Made Simple by David M. Greene

8

BUY A 2-4 FAMILY PROPERTY USING A VA, FHA, OR CONVENTIONAL LOAN.

If you want to build real wealth, start at home. The best real estate investments in America are 2-4 family properties. You live in one unit (for at least a year) and rent the other units.

Residential owner-occupied financing is the cheapest money you can find. A Federal Housing Administration (FHA) loan involves a down payment of only 3.5 percent, and even that amount can be gifted to you. The Veterans Administration (VA) loan involves no down payment. There are banks that will issue conventional loans for as little as 3 percent down.

The majority of people think that real estate is a good investment, yet many do not get started with investing because of a lack of capital. If you use an FHA loan to buy a triplex for

$400,000, the 3.5 percent down payment is only $14,000. With closing costs, you may only need $20,000 or a little more to buy it. If the triplex appreciates 5 percent in a year, that's another $20,000 of equity for you. Your $20,000 initial payment can produce cash flow, equity, and tax deductions for you for as long as you own the property.

The rent from the other units should cover most, if not all, of your mortgage payments. You will learn about property management. Tenants will be on their best behavior when they know the owner lives next door. You can save up money for the down payment on your next investment property.

If you see yourself living in a single-family home, sacrifice for at least a year and live in a 2-4 family property. Then move out and keep the multi-unit as an investment. You'll be glad you did.

9

NOT ALL FORECLOSURES ARE DEALS.

Many investors believe that they need to buy a foreclosure to get a deal. That is simplistic thinking.

Sure, many foreclosures are offered at a discount to fair market value. However, there can be multiple bidders on a foreclosure, and that could drive up the price. Many foreclosures have the utilities turned off, so it can be difficult to determine if the systems in the house function properly. Some banks will not allow a home inspection contingency, which means that an investor cannot back out of the contract without penalty if they find adverse inspection results. Banks are typically not required to disclose anything about the property, so you'll have to discover all the problems on your own.

Many foreclosures require more work than some investors can handle. I've made that mistake myself in my younger days—I ran out of money during the renovation because I underestimated the cost and scope of work. I had half-renovated properties sit vacant and quiet for months while I tried to come up with the money to finish the projects.

Some foreclosures are still occupied, and an investor may not be able to gain access until they evict the occupant after the property is purchased. I knew one investor who bought a house at a foreclosure auction, and it took 13 months to legally remove the occupant. The worst-ever case was that of Guramrit Hanspal, who made only one mortgage payment after buying his home in 1998. He then gamed the foreclosure and bankruptcy court systems to stay for 23 years without making a housing payment. The investors who bought the foreclosed house spent six figures on property taxes, insurance, and legal fees while Hanspal lived there for free.

Some bank asset managers overprice their foreclosures, leaving them to languish on the market.

Deals are everywhere. Foreclosures, homes for sale by owner, short sales, auctions, tax sales, and properties on the MLS all offer opportunity.

The truth is that some properties can be money pits. Foreclosures, homes for sale by owner, short sales, auctions, tax sales, and properties on the MLS can be more trouble than they're worth.

Look everywhere for deals. You reduce your risk and increase your profit when you know your numbers and your capabilities.

10

FIND THE DEALS HIDING IN PLAIN SIGHT ON THE MULTIPLE LISTING SERVICE.

Some investors believe that if a Realtor lists a property, then there's no way it can be a deal because everyone will see it. Just because a house is listed on the MLS does not mean that there will be competition for it. Some properties on the MLS are lucky to receive one offer—yours. Even if there are multiple offers for a house, your agent or the listing agent may be able to glean valuable information to give you the edge in negotiation. Some sellers don't want a lot of strangers traipsing through their house, so they may be willing to accept your offer the day the property is listed.

With a listed property, you can include a home inspection contingency. That allows you to back out of the deal if you find unacceptable inspection results. Armed with an inspection report and perhaps a contractor estimate, you can negotiate a credit or price reduction with the help of your agent. When buying my home, the inspection report noted that there was fungal growth in the crawl space. My wife and I obtained a $3,000 estimate to remove the old insulation, spray the joists with a special mold-killing solution, and install a vapor barrier plus new insulation. We emailed the inspection report and estimate to the listing agent. She shared them with her client. The seller agreed to pay the $3,000 if it could be taken out of her proceeds at the closing. We negotiated with the contractor to have them perform the work up front but wait a couple of weeks to be paid at the settlement. It worked out, and everyone was satisfied.

When you're under contract for a listed property, you have time to think. Typically, there is clearer and more frequent communication between the seller and buyer via their agents. Communication makes transactions go more smoothly.

Some properties on the MLS are listed over fair market value. Some are listed below fair market value. Sometimes paying the asking price nets you a great deal.

Some listed properties have been under contract multiple times, only to have the buyers back out. The seller may be fed up and ready to accept your offer just to get it over with. They might even give you the previous buyer's inspection report.

On the MLS, there are potential deals hiding in plain sight. Find them.

11
DO A SLOW FLIP ON YOUR OWN RESIDENCE.

The IRS tax code gives you a great gift. If you sold your primary residence and lived in it for two out of the last five years, then your first $250,000 of capital gains is tax-free if you are single. If married and filing jointly, then the first $500,000 of capital gains is tax-free.

The mortgage lenders give you a great gift. For owner-occupied homes, they offer the lowest down payments and the lowest interest rates.

The federal government gives you yet another great gift. There are government-backed mortgages. The U.S. Department of Agriculture (USDA) and VA loans allow eligible borrowers to purchase a home with no money down. A VA loan could even be used to buy a 2-4 unit residence. An FHA loan only requires a 3.5 percent down payment. Fannie Mae and Freddie Mac support the secondary housing market so lenders can give you lucrative loan terms.

If you need money to renovate a fixer-upper, consider the FHA 203k renovation loan, the Fannie Mae HomeStyle loan, and the Freddie Mac CHOICERenovation® loan. More gifts.

Buy your own home. Enjoy living in it. Improve it, especially if you purchased a fixer-upper. After at least two years, if you wish and if the value has gone up, sell it and buy another home.

If you prefer to keep the asset, buy a 2-4 family property. Live there for a while. Collect rent and learn to be a great landlord. If you wish to sell for a profit after a couple of years, do so. If you prefer to keep the asset and buy another one as your new personal residence, do that.

12
BUY THE LOSER IN THE NEIGHBORHOOD.

The worst house in a desirable neighborhood, at the right price, is a huge opportunity.

Identify what the detracting feature is, and then determine if it can be corrected. Is the house painted orange? Does excessive water drain onto the lot and up against the foundation? Is the interior dated? Is junk lying around the yard? Is it the only home without a view of the mountains?

If you can quickly and inexpensively correct the detracting feature, you will establish new appeal from buyers and renters. They will pay more. The higher values of the nearby homes will support your property's higher value.

13

DON'T GO OVER BUDGET.

Well-run businesses have a budget. Governments have a budget. You need a budget.

Don't pull a number out of thin air. Evaluate the scope of the project or the annual operating expenses. Consult with your contractors and advisors. Examine your finances.

If you're working on a flip project, see if you can bring a contractor to your showing or to your home inspection appointment. Sometimes contractors don't want to go to a showing because there's no guarantee that any offer you make will be accepted. It would be a waste of their time to prepare an estimate for a house you won't be able to buy. At least with your home inspection appointment, you're under contract to purchase the property and your inspector may find something that's worth pointing out to your contractor. If the contractor can't make it, take photos of the areas that need work. Share the photos and excerpts from the inspection report to ask for a price range. Ask your mentor to help you evaluate the scope of the renovation. Instead of paying for all new cabinets, what if you sanded them and painted them white? What if you stretched and shampooed the carpet instead of ripping it up and installing luxury vinyl planks?

If you're buying a rental property, ensure that you ask for every detail possible regarding the operating expenses for the past year. Ask for a copy of each lease. If the seller won't provide these details up front, make it a part of the purchase contract that they have no more than five days to supply you with the rent roll, expenses, and leases for your review. Many landlords don't have detailed expense numbers, so you may receive estimated amounts. If you receive pro-forma expense numbers, assume that they might be a little low.

Look at your capital and credit lines. Do you have the money to complete the renovations and cover unexpected costs? What if the renovation takes three months longer to complete than planned? What if the house takes four months longer to sell than you expected? What if the heating system fails right after you buy the property, and it's the middle of winter?

Once you establish your budget, track your numbers at least weekly. Strictly adhere to the budget. Act like the CEO of a major business who knows their company's numbers and pushes the entire organization to operate within the budget.

Financial discipline is planning well, tracking your numbers, and sticking to the monetary limits you set.

If you don't know your budget, you don't have one. Before you sign on the dotted line to buy a property, know your budget.

Then, stick to it. When formulating your budget, add a slight amount more for cost overruns or unanticipated expenses. You don't want to run out of money before your project is completed. A good rule of thumb for a renovation project is 15 percent more. For a rental property, keep a reserve account greater than your insurance deductible.

If you did set a budget, then you need to know where you are at any given time. Don't be one of those investors who has no clue how much they have spent on the deal. Tracking your income and expenses isn't hard. You just need a system to do it. The simpler, the better.

You don't want to play a game where you keep delaying payment to your contractors who completed their work. Your reputation will suffer.

A house flipper asked me to help him sell his house. I asked him how much money he had spent on the house and renovations. He had no idea. He said he would have to look at his receipts. I asked him where his receipts were. He had no idea.

What gets measured gets improved. Know your numbers. It's not hard to track numbers. It's simple math. Put all your receipts in one envelope. Each week, enter your numbers into accounting software or a spreadsheet. I use QuickBooks to track my income and expenses. If you have just one property, use Microsoft Excel or Google Sheets. For example, you can select an online template in Excel to create a business monthly budget in seconds. Instead of trying to create the spreadsheet from scratch, all you have to do is type in the amounts. If you're too busy to track expenses or you find Excel or Sheets overwhelming, hire a bookkeeper.

View a tight budget as a challenge. A strict budget forces you and your team to be creative and learn new ways of doing things. Rather than throw more money at a problem, throw the full weight of your team's inventiveness and ingenuity at it.

14

BUY BACK YOUR TIME.

The best CEOs don't ask themselves, "How can I do this?" The best CEOs ask, "Who can do this?"

What is your time worth? $15 per hour? $25 per hour? $100? $200? More?

Just because you can do repair work does not mean you should do it. I can clean my own home, yet I pay someone else $25 an hour to do it. That person is better at it than me, and my time is better spent on activities that produce much more than $25 per hour. Cleaning drains my physical and mental energy since I don't enjoy it as much as other things.

In my younger days, I did all the interior painting for my investment properties. I felt, for some reason, that painters were too expensive. I felt that painting required low skill, and therefore I believed that I would save money by doing it myself. While I was saving money in terms of not paying someone to paint, I cost myself time with my family, time for physical fitness, time for other income generating activities, and time for thinking about how to grow my business. Today, I pay a painter $20 per hour to handle our investment properties. He loves painting and does a great job.

We use leverage in so many areas of our lives without even thinking about it. When you dine at a restaurant, they prepare the table, cook the food, and clean up afterward for you. You buy tomatoes at the grocery store when you could have grown them in your yard. You have the postal service send a package for you instead of you driving it to the recipient yourself.

By paying $25 an hour for a house cleaner or $20 an hour for a painter, I am buying back my time. There are only so many hours in a day. By strategically using leverage in my business and my personal life, I can spend more time with family and dear friends. That time is priceless. I find that I get more satisfaction out of life by stripping things off my to-do list, not adding things on.

You are the CEO of your own business. You make the decisions on who to hire and who to fire. You pick your contractors, your accountant, your attorney, your Realtor, your insurance agent, and so on. Imagine that you have a Board of Directors holding you accountable as the CEO. (In reality, you should have someone holding you accountable in your business.) So if the CEO spends more time each day performing $15 per hour activities and less time on $200 per hour activities, what would the Board ultimately do? They probably would fire the CEO for failing to focus on what maximizes the growth of the business.

Your business grows to the extent that you do. You cannot build a big business without leverage. Ask, "Who can do this?"

15

KNOW THE AFTER REPAIR VALUE BEFORE YOU MAKE AN OFFER.

Real estate doesn't have to be a guessing game. It can be highly predictable. When you evaluate an opportunity, you need to know the After Repair Value (ARV), the renovation costs, the closing costs, and the cost of your financing. A contractor can give you a renovation estimate and how long it will take to do the job. A Realtor or title agency can calculate your closing costs. Your lender can tell you about their fees and rates.

Let's examine the ARV formula:

ARV = Property's current value + Renovation costs + Sweat equity

Many investors define the ARV as the current value plus renovation expenses. However, that calculation does not factor in the additional value that a buyer or appraiser may see in an updated home. For example, if the current value is $150,000 and renovation costs are $50,000, that doesn't mean the ARV will be $200,000 (unless you paid too much for the property at $150,000). The ARV could be $275,000, meaning that your $50,000 of improvements actually increased the value by $125,000. Therefore, your hard work (sweat equity) created an extra $75,000 of value.

A sharp investor quickly evaluates many potential deals they see online before getting in their vehicle to see the ones that made the initial cut. You may view 100 properties online yet only physically look at 10. So how do you come up with the ARV?

Many people look for the Zillow Zestimate, also available as the Trulia Estimate (Zillow owns Trulia). Realtor.com provides a home value on most houses from up to three sources, which are CoreLogic, Quantarium, and Collateral Analytics.

Even though you may glean some values from Zillow and Realtor.com, those numbers do not always represent the ARV. One challenge for these algorithms is that the condition of the property is not really known. Another challenge is that the algorithms may not know certain factors that could enhance or diminish the value. For instance, if a house has walk-through bedrooms, the algorithm will not know that and could value the property higher than it should be. The Zillow and Realtor.com valuations help you establish a value range more so than a specific value.

A Realtor's comparable market analysis (CMA) carries a lot of weight. A Realtor, particularly one who has seen the property virtually or in person, can factor in recent sales, the layout, the location, and other factors.

Knowing the ARV will protect you from making a huge mistake. Go to Zillow and Realtor.com to see their algorithm-based valuations. Talk to your Realtor. Befriend an appraiser. Find out what nearby houses recently sold for.

When renovating the property, ensure that your upgrades are similar to or slightly better than the comparable sales you evaluated.

16

TAKE TIME TO DEVELOP YOUR BUSINESS STRATEGY.

"Thinking is the hardest work there is, which is probably the reason why so few engage in it." - Henry Ford

In the long run, the strategist always defeats the tactician.

Tactical approach: Work harder.

Strategic approach: Work smarter.

Play the long game, not the short game. Instead of looking for a 6-month payoff, act as if there is an infinite upside. Most people overestimate what they can accomplish in one year and underestimate what they can accomplish in 10 years.

The strategist wonders, "How can I maximize every resource at my disposal?"

A tactical landlord finds the deal, buys the renovation materials, fixes the house, and self-manages the tenants. There is a limit on how many units and tenants they can manage.

A strategic landlord studies the types of financing and seeks to maximize their rate of return. A strategic landlord establishes specific criteria for finding deals, and they enlist help in finding and negotiating deals. They hire others to do the renovation and repair work. They hire a proven property management team to deal with tenants and suggest ways to increase revenue. There is no limit on how many units they can acquire.

99 percent of entrepreneurs are tactical. To make more money, they believe they must work more hours and sell more widgets.

0.8 percent of entrepreneurs are strategic. They are big thinkers who are not concerned with details.

0.2 percent of entrepreneurs are strategic and tactical. They have big ideas and piercing implementation. They ask, "Who can do this?" instead of, "How can I do this?" They develop policies and procedures that others can follow. They create written systems. They leverage their business through people and systems.

To be more strategic, spend an hour a day thinking. Think about the market trends. Is there a shortage of housing in your area? Is the population growing? Are banks loosening their lending standards and providing low interest loans? Is there a new Chick-fil-A or Starbucks being built nearby? Major companies perform extensive market research, and they would only establish a new location if the demographics and traffic support it.

Think about how to employ more leverage. Is there a reliable handyman you can hire? What about a bookkeeper, grass cutter, house cleaner, property manager, or Realtor? Leverage does not just include people. It includes software and systems. If you're self-managing your rentals, could you use special software for tenants to place maintenance requests and pay you electronically? When researching market rents, I save time by using the Pro version of RentOMeter.com and by reviewing the free Zillow Rent Zestimate.

Think about how to improve your skills. Should you obtain a real estate license? What educational seminar or investor group should you attend?

Think about where you want your business to be in one year, ten years, and thirty years. When do you want to stop working a day job? Where do you want to live? What lifestyle do you wish to enjoy? What will be your legacy?

Think about how to upgrade your team's results. Is there a coach or mentor who can help you turn years into months by helping you accelerate your results? Thinking is the hardest work there is.

Ask yourself, "How do my tactical efforts help me with my strategy?" If your strategic result is to have more free time yet you keep acquiring rental units that you self-manage, then you need to consider hiring a property manager. Also ask, "What is the strategic result of each tactical effort?" If your goal is to build passive income that exceeds your living expenses but all you do is flip houses, then you need to keep some houses to rent out.

17

DON'T CHANGE COURSE MID-STREAM.

A novice investor bought a fixer-upper. When asked what they were going to do with it, they said, "I don't know. When it's fixed up, I may sell it. Or if it doesn't sell, I'll rent it. Maybe I'll advertise it for sale *and* rent and see what happens."

A flipper typically improves a fixer-upper to a higher standard than a landlord. A flipper might provide brand-new appliances, whereas a landlord might install used appliances or keep the ones that came with the house. A flipper might install granite countertops, while a landlord may simply clean the existing Formica. A flipper might pay less for a fixer-upper than a landlord, as the flipper will probably spend more on renovations and needs to factor in their profit. A landlord may spend less on renovations, instead prioritizing cash flow.

When searching for a property to buy, a landlord may have more neighborhoods to choose from. A flipper may only seek out up-and-coming residential neighborhoods. A residential property on the fringe of a commercial area might not be a good flip, yet it could be well suited as a rental. A flipper and a landlord might even select different types of financing.

Before you make an offer for a property, know your exit strategy. Don't change course mid-stream. An investor who simultaneously lists their renovated property for sale and rent does not know what they want. When you do not know what you want, what you get is less profit.

18

BUY CLOSE TO HOME.

Buy investment properties within 45 minutes, preferably less, than where you live. I bought my first property 100 miles from where I lived, and the next day I bought my second property 45 miles away. The two properties were in opposite directions. I had to interview and manage contractors in both locations. Even easy tasks were incredibly time-consuming. Checking on progress at the properties was difficult. I wasted money on gas and tolls. I made dozens of trips just to show each place to prospective tenants, and some didn't even show up.

Buy close to home. The deals are out there. You just need to look for them. As you develop reliable contractors, you can use them on all your properties instead of having to build up multiple networks. Your network can even become a free sales force, constantly keeping their eyes and ears open for the next deal that you may consider.

When you purchase near where you live, you will come to know the neighborhoods and property values well. You reduce your risk when you are highly familiar with the area.

You will save time and money buying close to home. Even if far-flung properties seem like they can be purchased for a lot less, remember that your time and mental health are worth a lot too.

19

CREATE A FREE SALES FORCE.

One of the best ways to find deals is through word of mouth. When neighbors, friends, family, co-workers, contractors, or fellow churchgoers see or hear of a fixer-upper or motivated seller, they can tell you about it. You need to teach them how.

Some companies pay millions of dollars for their sales force. You can have one for free.

Train your sales force on how to refer business. Tell them to call you right away when they come across a potential deal. Don't have them simply give a potential seller your name and number. There is a greater than 90 percent chance that the potential seller will not call you, even if they promised your friend they would. The better way is to have your friend tell the potential seller they'll have you call them. Tell your friend to inform you right away. This ensures that there will be a 100 percent chance that you'll call the prospect.

Reward your sales force for every referral, not just if you buy the property. It can be as simple as a thank you note with a $5 gift card to a coffee shop.

20

DON'T USE ALL YOUR CREDIT ON A DEAL, ESPECIALLY IF YOUR BUSINESS PARTNER IS NOT USING THEIRS.

A person with bad credit may seek to partner with someone with good credit. Do not buy real estate or renovation materials using your own credit if your business partner does not utilize their credit. If you have good credit and your associate uses your credit lines, you take on more risk than they are. If you must place a personal guarantee on a loan and they do not, there is an even greater imbalance of risk. You should reconsider whether you need your partner at all.

In my first business partnership many years ago, I signed contracts and mortgage paperwork to buy a house in my name and then transferred the ownership to an LLC co-owned by two other partners. One of my partners leased the property to less-than-stellar tenants who stopped paying rent. Their aggressive dog bit the neighbor's daughter, and that neighbor turned out to be a judge. The judge notified the city code enforcement office, who promptly condemned the property. The tenants left the house unsecured with a broken window on the rear door, and the city enforced the condemnation because the house was "vacant and unsecured." I had to deal with a bevy of angry code enforcement officers who scrutinized the premises and listed everything they could that required upgrades. I spent thousands of dollars just to pull the house out of condemnation status. In retrospect, I did not need my partners and could have done that deal and others without them.

I entered another partnership in which a partner recently declared bankruptcy but did not tell me about it. He insisted upon overseeing the company's money. We created entities and used my credit for company credit cards. All the credit lines were eventually maxed out, and then payments stopped being made. I exited the partnership and had to settle with the creditors. In retrospect, I did not need my partners and could have built a business without them.

When entering a partnership, conduct a thorough background check on all the prospective partners. You evaluate potential tenants to determine whether they should have access to your property. It is even more important to evaluate potential partners because they may end up having access to far more than a rental unit.

21

DON'T ADD UNNECESSARY PARTNERS.

Don't add unnecessary partners to a deal or, worse, to a company.

Sometimes investors feel lonely and want their friends to be a part of an adventure, so they encourage them to join the deal. This is a way to lose some friends. If you feel the need to bring someone along for the ride, let them live vicariously through you. Take them to lunch, share your ideas, and seek their thoughts. But don't make them partners.

Some people bring on a partner to reduce fear or compensate for a perceived weakness. They give up 50 percent or more of their future profits and majority control of their business in exchange for feeling a little better. Hire a coach instead and have a great mentor—you'll spend less than 50 percent of the profit and have total control of your business.

You may be able to find a mentor at a local real estate investing club or perhaps even through your church, workplace, neighborhood, or family. As for a coach, ask fellow investors who they work with and also conduct research online. Do not pay a coach a massive sum up front. Years ago, I attended a free weekend investor workshop in Manhattan. It turned out to be a manipulative setup for overpriced coaching programs. The organizers pitched me on a $59,995 coaching program and said that if I signed up on the spot, they would cut the price to $29,995. They had several salesmen call me for weeks on end trying to sign me up. The program consisted of weekly 30-minute calls with a coach from another state. There's nothing wrong with virtual coaching, yet if you have $29,995 most of it should go into your deal.

In addition to their strengths, partners also bring their weaknesses. You typically don't discover their weaknesses until you encounter problems with the deal or the company.

If you are an equal partner or a minority partner with someone, that person can obligate the business. He or she can spend your money, hire their people, and fire your people. He or she can bring in a different set of standards than you have, and that will create conflict. You'll spend more time seething or fighting and less time earning.

If you are afraid of making colossal mistakes, your advisors will protect you. Periodically consult your coach, mentor, legal counsel, and tax advisor. Then you, and you alone, make the decisions and keep the profit.

Only bring in a partner if they have a proven track record of success and can add immediate value. Work with them on one or two deals first before making them a member of your company.

22

YOU GET WHAT YOU TOLERATE.

If a business relationship is not working, get out sooner rather than later. If the contractor is not the right fit, do not keep hiring them for additional jobs.

You teach people how to treat you. If any of your team members or vendors ignore you or disrespect you, then have a candid conversation with them about expectations. Sometimes a small conflict, resolved in an empowering way, builds trust. If they change their behavior and you believe they will be a good fit going forward, continue building the relationship. If their behavior remains beneath your standards, then find better people.

You get what you inspect, not what you expect. You must periodically inspect your renovation projects, your financials, and your insurance policies. If you hire contractors, they and their subcontractors must know that you keep a watchful eye on the premises. If you hire employees, they must know that you keep a watchful eye on the business.

23

DO NOT PARTNER WITH A CONTRACTOR WHO SAYS THEY'LL DO THE RENOVATION WORK.

Hire a contractor, yes. Partner with a contractor, no. Do not partner with a contractor who says their contribution will be to conduct the renovations.

Contractors focus on the jobs that make them money now, so your project will always be last.

As a young man, I partnered with a contractor. Using my money, I bought the property and put his name on the deed along with my company's name. His job was to supply the materials and perform the work by a certain deadline that he agreed to meet. We were going to flip the house and split the profit 50-50. Unfortunately, we went months past the deadline. The contractor only did work when he had time off from his customers' jobs. The few materials he bought were substandard or even items removed from old houses. He kept telling me that he would go work on the house tomorrow. Tomorrow never came. Eventually I had to pay him thousands of dollars to remove his name from the deed. I would have been far better off buying the property myself and hiring a different contractor.

24

HOW TO EVALUATE A CONTRACTOR BEFORE HIRING THEM.

When considering a contractor you have not worked with, ask for proof of their license. Verify it by calling the governmental authority that issued it.

Ask for proof of insurance. Verify it by calling the insurer.

Ask if the contractor marks up for materials costs. If they buy $700 of lumber, they shouldn't tell you that they paid $1,300 for it. To prevent markups and only pay for labor, you could purchase the materials per the contractor's specifications and have them delivered to the job site or have the contractor pick them up from the hardware store's Will Call. It's reasonable if the contractor charges a nominal fee to order and pick up materials.

Ask to speak with one of their past customers. Invariably the contractor will give you the contact information of someone who will say good things about them. Nevertheless, your conversation with the past customer may help you make an informed decision. Ask them if the contractor completed the job when they said they would. Ask if the contractor responded to every single call and text message. Ask how the other employees or subcontractors behaved on the job site.

You can ask to see photos of the contractor's past handiwork. Unscrupulous contractors may show you photos of someone else's work. After you are given photos, ask for the address where the work was conducted. Then look on Google Maps, Zillow, or Realtor.com to see if the photos you were given match up with the online photos of that property.

The more money you give to a contractor up front, the less leverage you have and the more risk you absorb. Few contractors will start work without a deposit. It is reasonable for a contractor to ask for an initial payment to buy materials, prepare drawings, and pull permits. That initial payment should not be more than 33 percent of the total job estimate.

If a contractor asks for 50 percent (or perhaps even all) of the money up front to start work, respond by saying, "I'm not comfortable with paying 50 percent—50 percent!—upfront. How can I be made more comfortable?"

Don't pay a contractor more than one-third of the money upfront; certainly don't give the contractor additional money if they haven't done the work. Ensure the contractor states in writing when the job will start and when it will finish. On a big job, as for an email or text message at the beginning of each week on the contractor's goals for your project that week.

When the job is done, inspect the work. If you are not satisfied, explain specifically what could be improved. When you are satisfied, pay the remaining balance promptly.

25

START YOUR RENOVATION PROJECT THE MOMENT YOU BUY THE PROPERTY.

Time is money. Inertia is costly. As the ink is drying on the closing paperwork, work should be starting at your property. Even if it is simply a handyman removing some junk, get the job started right away.

What you know in advance, you can do in advance. If you know you are buying a house on September 26th, then have the handyman scheduled to start on the 26th. Schedule your settlements for early in the day so you have a full day to get things done at the property. At a recent purchase, my wife and I were at the closing table at 9:30 a.m. Our handyman was at the property waiting for me to call him to say that he could start work. We had construction materials scheduled to be delivered that day.

Don't think, "I'll get to it when I get to it." Your fixer-upper properties should be bustling with activity. Your contractors and vendors must know you are a serious businessperson who runs a tight ship.

A novice flipper called me recently to seek advice on buying a second property. I asked about the first house. He said that he had been working on it for three years, and it was far from finished. I advised him to put all his resources into renovating and selling the first house. He eventually completed that first house and sold it. A flip of a single-family home should not take over three years unless you are using it as your primary residence in the meantime.

Put energy into your renovation projects. Your contractors should expect to see you around the job site at least a couple times a week. If you're a landlord and the potential monthly rent is $3,000, that's $100 in income you're losing every day the unit stays vacant. When you factor in taxes, insurance, and utilities, the unrented unit could be costing you $150 or more per day.

Let's say you are a flipper who makes about $40,000 a sale. Not only should you consider the daily cost of carrying the property, but you must also factor in the opportunity cost of not doing another flip because of inertia on your current project. Think about the velocity of your money. If your construction project had not taken so long, you could have completed another flip project that year with the same capital. That may have produced another $40,000 in profit.

Push yourself and your team to get the job done.

26

CREATE SO MUCH VALUE FOR YOUR CONTRACTORS THAT THEY PUT YOUR NEEDS FIRST.

When your project has numerous delays because contractors are working elsewhere, it's a sign that you need to add more value to your relationships. Vendors prioritize who they work for based on who gives them the most value.

Sometimes value is measured by who pays most, but not always. Value can be created by paying promptly when the job is done. Value can be giving a bonus when the job is done exceptionally well or completed ahead of schedule. Value can be remembering the contractor's birthday or anniversary. It is remembering the names of the subcontractors and the contractor's kids.

Value can be buying pizzas for the work crew just because. Value is created through empowering conversations, especially when things aren't going according to plan.

Value is created through referrals. When you give plenty of business to a vendor, they see you not just as a customer but also as a growth partner.

Constantly seek to provide value to your contractors. They will find ways to return value to you.

27

DON'T FIGHT CITY HALL.

A code enforcement officer can wield tremendous power over your project. Get to know how the permit system works. Ensure the necessary permits are obtained. Go to the code enforcement office before you purchase your first property in that area. Mention that you're thinking of buying an investment property and ask how the process works.

I had a great working relationship with the head of the code enforcement office in Allentown, Pennsylvania. When I was under contract to buy an apartment building, I stopped by to ask him about it. He looked in his computer and said, "Our records show that the building burned down nine days ago." I was shocked. The seller had not told me that the building burned. I terminated that contract.

Be compliant, polite, and detailed with your communications. Build a reputation so that the entire code enforcement office knows that you're one of the good ones.

A solid relationship with the city is worth a lot of money. You won't know it until you encounter a problem. If you do encounter a problem, don't fight City Hall. To be angry with the right person at the right time in the right way is difficult to pull off. Chances are you will create more problems than solutions.

If you are flipping houses, expect buyers to inquire whether the proper permits were pulled. You don't want your sale to be jeopardized or your reputation with the city tarnished if someone calls you out for failing to pull permits.

You reduce your liability when you ensure that electrical, plumbing, and other required work is performed to the city's standards.

As a landlord, do not allow your unit to be occupied by more people than the maximum number permitted by the city.

28

DON'T CUT CORNERS ON RENOVATIONS, AND DON'T OVER-IMPROVE PROPERTIES EITHER.

Do what it takes to get it done right, and don't do more than that. A property should be clean, neat, and sturdy, in line with the neighborhood and price bracket.

Novice investors can get carried away with over-improving a property. After all, it can be a joy to transform a fixer-upper into a modern marvel. Yet the top-of-the line improvements should be saved for your home and not necessarily an investment property. Your budget is the limiting factor.

Some investors cut so many corners that they put lipstick on a pig. Trying to hide blemishes and fool your buyer or renter is bad business. I knew an investor who spray-painted a roof black to make it appear new. He told the buyers of his flip house not to work with a Realtor. He told the unsuspecting buyers they did not need a home inspection since the city had already inspected the house, and it "passed." He sold the buyers a house with a non-functioning heat system in the middle of winter and then told them that they should contact the home warranty company to get the heat system operating.

Many landlords will choose not to improve a dwelling to the same level as a house flipper might, and that's fine. The bottom line is that you should do the job right.

29

CHANGE THE LOCKS.

Countless stories exist of stolen items with unforced entry. It's simple to change the locks. Most of the time, you can do it yourself. Change the locks as soon as you buy a property. Change the locks right before a new tenant moves in.

Save the salvageable locksets and use them on another property. Or, pay a little more and buy the locksets that can be rekeyed. Another option is to have a lock with a programmable code.

You reduce your liability and prevent theft when you change the locks. Tell your tenant when they move in that you just changed the locks. Security is the number one concern tenants have, and they will appreciate that they have new locks.

If one of the roommates moves away after a falling out with the other roommate(s), offer to change the locks or code. It's better for the landlord to always maintain control of the locks instead of the tenants installing their own. When tenants change the locks, they often buy the cheapest ones and fail to give a key to the landlord. Then the landlord cannot access their own property if there is a maintenance need or emergency.

30

DEAl WITH THE ROOF FIRST.

The roof protects everything underneath it. Don't let water undo all your hard work.

A real estate investor borrowed $2 million to purchase and renovate an empty 18-unit building. The flat roof was leaking when he bought the property, so he patched some areas himself. He then installed high-end light fixtures, granite countertops, stainless steel appliances, a new elevator, and many other luxurious features. He spent every dollar of his loan making the interior look like a Manhattan hotel. He rented all 18 units. Then the roof started leaking again. The water repeatedly set off the fire alarm for the whole building. The investor could not afford to replace the roof. After several visits by the fire department, the city condemned the building, and all the tenants had to move out. The bank foreclosed on the building.

Had the investor replaced the roof upfront and spent a little less on the interior renovations, he would have stayed within his means and been able to keep the fully rented building.

31

COMPLETE YOUR RENOVATION PROJECT BEFORE JUMPING TO THE NEXT ONE.

Jimmy, the general contractor from Wilkes-Barre, Pennsylvania, has been in business for over 40 years and is still going. Jimmy has a crew of six people. They work big jobs for the local hospitals and smaller jobs for the landlords and homeowners in the area. Jimmy has run his business with a simple philosophy all these years: Put all your resources into one job, finish it, and then start the next job. Jimmy will tell customers that he cannot start their job for another six weeks, and the customers are happy to wait because they know that Jimmy will be there 100 percent when he does begin. Jobs are done well and done quickly.

Where focus goes, energy flows. Jimmy's crew is not running from job site to job site, trying to remember where they left their tools. Customers are not left to wonder if the workers are showing up today. Jimmy is not mentally overwhelmed by trying to deal with problems from multiple projects all at once. His employees work as a team under the watchful eye of the boss.

Many lousy general contractors are quick to take deposits from new customers while promising that they'll start work right away. They take on too many jobs, perhaps because they see dollar signs in their eyes or fear the customer will go elsewhere. These contractors are constantly running around trying to stave off customer complaints while their employees stand around and barely work.

Be like Jimmy. Focus your resources on finishing a renovation project completely. Then focus on the next one. While it may seem like you are moving slower toward accomplishing your goals, you'll actually move along faster.

32

GET IT IN WRITING.

A written agreement protects each party. Even a simple agreement with a laborer should be in writing if the job costs more than $300.

A novice investor hired two men to install vinyl siding materials that the investor had purchased. They verbally agreed upon a price of $7,000 to be paid upon completion of the work. On the first Friday after work began, the installers showed up at the investor's place of work to demand payment since Easter Sunday was that weekend. The investor felt annoyance and sympathy, so he paid the men $2,000 and told them that the remaining $5,000 would be paid upon completion of the job. The following Friday, men showed up at the investor's workplace again to demand another payment since Mother's Day was that weekend, and they needed to buy gifts for Mom. The investor again paid $2,000, telling the men that the remaining $3,000 would be paid upon completion of the job. The men showed up again the following Friday, saying they needed their "weekly salary" of $2,000. By not having a written agreement and not saying "no," the investor created the conditions for misunderstandings and frustration on both sides.

33

WALK THE JOB SITE AT LEAST TWICE A WEEK.

On a renovation or construction project, walk the job site at least twice a week. Don't try to manage a project from the other side of your desk. Don't hide behind your cellphone. Don't assume that things are going according to plan.

Get out there and see what the contractors are doing. Ensure that they are not using substandard materials. Make sure the colors match. See if you want to upgrade anything else while the walls are open. Learn about your property. You'll become better at spotting issues with future properties.

I checked on a renovation project in which the general contractor was remodeling the entire kitchen. The first time I walked through, I didn't notice anything amiss with the new white cabinets. The second time, right before the countertops were installed, I saw it. One of the base cabinets was a different design than all the others. I sent a photo to the boss. He immediately had his crew replace the mismatched base cabinet with the right one.

When the contractors know you stop by frequently, they are more likely to arrive on time. They will work harder since the owner is there. They will consult with you more. It will become apparent which contractors you should continue to do business with.

Meet the neighbors. They are your allies. They observe a lot. They can keep an eye on your property. They may be the source of your next deal.

Some contractors will offer to send photos or perform a video call. That's helpful. However, things can be missed because the contractor is only showing you what they see or want you to see. There is no substitute for you physically being there.

Every time you walk the job site, you will learn something new.

34

CONVERT A 4/1 INTO A 3/2.

If you buy a 4-bedroom, 1-bathroom house, convert it into a 3-bedroom, 2-bathroom house. This principle applies regardless of whether you are a flipper or landlord. If you can create a master suite if there isn't one already, that adds value.

If you are a landlord, in your market there is likely a larger pool of renters for a 3-bedroom unit versus a 4-bedroom unit. If your rental only has one bathroom and there is a problem with a clogged toilet or malfunctioning shower, you may have to pay extra to rush a plumber out there. If the renters have a second bathroom, it's not as much of an emergency. The tenants are more likely to lease the home for a long time because of the convenience of a second bathroom.

If you are a flipper, you typically have a larger pool of potential buyers for a 3/2 house versus a 4/1 house. The second bathroom adds a lot of value to the buyer's and appraiser's eyes, especially if there is a master suite.

35

WHEN FLIPPING AN ENTRY-LEVEL HOUSE, WAIT 90 DAYS BEFORE PUTTING IT ON THE MARKET.

When fixing and flipping a house, every day counts. Insurance, taxes, utilities, and mortgage interest add up. Speed matters.

One exception allows you to have up to 90 days to methodically handle your renovation, and that is on entry-level homes (typically those priced under $300,000 in many markets). About one-third of buyers of starter homes may use an FHA loan. FHA has an anti-flipping provision, which states that an FHA loan can only be allowed if the seller has owned the property for at least 90 days.

Here is the timeline:

Day 0: Purchase the house.

Days 1 to 85: Renovate the house.

Day 86: Stage the house, if desired.

Day 87: Have your Realtor take photos.

Day 91: Have your Realtor place the house on the market.

By waiting 90 days, your house will be desired by a larger pool of buyers. FHA buyers have fewer options to choose from, so let them compete for your house. Even if you accept an offer from a non-FHA buyer, it's possible that the FHA buyers interested in your house will have created a competitive situation to drive your price up.

Another advantage is that with 90 days, you don't need to cut corners. You can be methodical with your work. You have time to shop around for the best prices on materials. You may even save money on contractors because you're not paying a premium to have them do the work immediately. You will have more time with your family or to work on other projects.

36

KNOW YOUR TRUE FINANCIAL PICTURE.

My wife and I knew the exact day we became millionaires. We even predicted that day in advance because we knew our numbers.

Know your true financial picture. Update it at least once a month. Be organized with your bookkeeping. Track your net worth. Know the difference between a Balance Sheet (assets and liabilities) and an Income Statement (income and expenses). What gets measured gets improved.

A CEO of a major corporation knows how to read financial statements. You should too. A sharp businessperson can predict even before the quarter is over how the company has performed and how it will perform in the next period.

I know too many entrepreneurs who judge their business based merely on how much they have in their bank accounts. They go to their accountant at tax time and ask, "How did we do last year?" Your accountant should not be telling you how the company did; you should be telling your accountant how the company did.

Keep a personal Balance Sheet, which is your net worth. It's fun and simple and will motivate you to continue growing your wealth. If you have Microsoft Excel, when creating a new file there are several free online profit and loss/income statement and balance sheet/net worth templates available. A simple Google search will likewise yield multiple resources already made for you.

37

IF YOUR CREDIT SCORE IS NOT WHERE IT NEEDS TO BE, GET IT THERE AS FAST AS POSSIBLE.

If your credit score is not where it needs to be, get it there. Consider hiring a credit restoration service. Make sure it is a legitimate company.

FICO score ranges are Poor (350-579), Fair (580-669), Good (670-739), Very Good (740-799), and Exceptional (800-850). I was in the Exceptional range when I started as a real estate investor. During the Great Recession, I collapsed to the Poor category. With focused effort over time, I returned to the Exceptional range and have stayed there ever since.

A FICO score is impacted by five factors, each with their own weighting. Payment History accounts for 35 percent of the credit score calculation. Amounts Owed is 30 percent of the score.

Length of Credit History makes up 15 percent. Credit Mix covers 10 percent of the score. New Credit makes up the remaining 10 percent.

When my FICO score was 450, these are the actions I took to reach 800:

- Used Rental Kharma to have my landlord report my timely rent payments to a credit bureau.
- Read Dave Ramsey's *The Total Money Makeover: A Proven Plan for Financial Fitness* and used his Debt Snowball method to pay off each debt starting with the smallest balance.
- Paid a one-time fee to a credit restoration service, which sent letters to the three credit bureaus asking to expunge certain items on my credit report.
- Agreed to settlement payments with creditors willing to accept a lump sum payoff.
- Set up payment plans with the remaining creditors.
- Modified my mortgage loan to reduce my monthly payments.
- Worked hard and earned bonuses at my day job.
- Added income streams to earn more money to pay down debt.

With terrible credit, you can still invest in real estate and even borrow money. However, you should stack the deck in your favor. Give yourself every advantage you can in the real estate game. Money is easier and cheaper when your credit score is high.

If your income is not where it needs to be, get it there. Create so much value for your employer that they are forced to pay you more.

If you wish to switch careers, talk with your mortgage loan originator first to see how the change may affect your ability to borrow.

38

KNOW AND USE THE LEGITIMATE TAX DEDUCTIONS AND EXEMPTIONS.

People like to complain about the government. They're entitled to their opinion. Instead of complaining, study all the ways the government gives you tax breaks. Read books. Talk to your accountant more than once a year. Pick the brain of someone much wealthier than you. Consult your attorney. Create an entity if advisable.

Have a separate business account or credit card to easily track your expenses. Don't commingle personal and business accounts. For our rental properties, my wife and I have one account for security deposits since those funds do not technically belong to us. We have another account for receiving rent and paying expenses. We have a personal bank account for our family expenses. We own a real estate brokerage that has an escrow account and an operating account. We have two rewards credit cards for keeping expenses segregated. We have a debit card for each of our operating accounts.

Consider changing your personal residence to a state with no personal income tax. My wife and I moved to Tennessee, which has no state personal income tax.

Track your mileage or let your entity own or lease your car. I use the MileIQ app to easily log business miles.

Pay yourself a salary. My real estate brokerage pays a salary to my wife and me.

Put money in a traditional Individual Retirement Account (IRA) and a Health Savings Account (HSA). My wife and I each have a traditional IRA. We also have an HSA. The amounts invested each year are tax deductible.

If you have a kid over the age of 7, pay him or her to work for the business. If your meal has a business purpose, expense it.

We sold rental real estate in one state and bought rental properties in another state. We conducted a 1031 tax-deferred exchange via a qualified intermediary, which means that we indefinitely deferred the payment of capital gains tax.

If you sell your principal residence and you lived in it at least two out of the last five years, then your first $250,000 of capital gains are tax free (up to $500,000 of capital gains are tax free if you are married, filing jointly).

If you mortgage your real estate, you can deduct much, if not all, of your loan interest. So even if you pay interest, you can claim tax deductions while investing that capital elsewhere. My wife and I shopped around and obtained low-interest loans on some of our real estate, while we chose to own some properties free and clear for the cash flow. When we did borrow money, we used it to buy additional assets that produce passive income.

Use the tax advantages the government gives you.

39

FILE YOUR TAXES ON TIME.

Don't procrastinate on filing your tax returns. File by the standard deadline and only file for an extension under extenuating circumstances. Be neat and complete.

If you need help with bookkeeping, pay for it. If you don't handle your books well, you will pay for it later in late fees to creditors, tax penalties, higher interest rates, extra hours charged by your accountant to play detective, and maybe even embezzlement by an opportunistic employee. Bookkeeping software is sophisticated enough to pull transactions straight from your bank and credit card accounts.

Pay your taxes in advance throughout the year as dictated by the IRS and your tax preparer. Do not ever fail to pay your taxes. The IRS has extraordinary powers, and they do not go away just because you ignore them. There will be challenges when you operate a business, and the IRS should not be one of them.

If you want a business or mortgage loan, you need up-to-date tax returns and an Income Statement. Don't hamper the growth of your business and investments because you put off filing your taxes.

40

DON'T CREATE TOO MANY ENTITIES.

Complexity is the enemy of execution. Keep your business simple. There is nothing wrong with creating an entity to take title in a property and give you additional liability protection. However, unless you run a conglomerate, you will not need dozens of entities.

My first attorney told me, "Don't ever ask a lawyer if you need a lawyer because the answer will always be 'Yes.'" Listen to your attorney's advice, and remember you are the boss. Explore your options thoroughly when considering the creation of yet another entity to hold real estate.

Each entity you create will need to file federal and state tax returns. You'll keep your accountant busy and your accounting bills high. Your banker will like opening lots of accounts for you, and you will get confused at the hardware store checkout with all the debit and credit cards in your billfold.

If you want to protect your assets, consider an umbrella policy to provide extra insurance coverage. Look into legal protection insurance. The best legal insurance includes free consultations with attorneys on a variety of topics, from getting out of a speeding ticket to reviewing a contract.

Commercial financing for companies is more expensive than financing in your own name. Loan terms are generally less favorable for an entity, even if you personally guarantee the money.

Run your business lean and mean. You should be able to explain your business structure to an 8-year-old and have them understand it.

41

PAY FOR LEGAL INSURANCE.

When many people should consult an attorney, they choose not to because they don't want to pay for an hour or two of the attorney's time. They end up costing themselves even more.

When many people finally hire an attorney, the situation is a mess that largely could have been prevented with wise counsel beforehand.

Some companies provide legal insurance, also known as pre-paid legal plans, for less than a dollar per day. With such a service, you can call upon a lawyer for any of many matters at no extra charge. For many situations, a 15-minute conversation with an attorney will give you the confidence to know the next step. Typically, the first letter from the attorney is included. Sometimes a mere letter from a law firm will make the other party accommodate your need.

I have been a subscriber to Legal Shield since 2005. I have spoken with their provider attorneys dozens of times through the years. The advice I received has given me an edge in negotiations and in resolving issues. The letters sent by attorneys on my behalf have been valuable. Only once in 18 years did Legal Shield increase my monthly fee.

If you are ever sued, legal insurance gives you an edge over the other party. They must spend money to pursue the lawsuit while you have a head start.

42

DON'T SIGN UP FOR TOO MANY SUBSCRIPTION SERVICES, OR THE MONTHLY FEES WILL EAT YOU ALIVE.

In business, the death of a thousand cuts comes from seemingly small expenses that drain your bank account dry every month. Entire industries exist—including spammers—that attempt to convince real estate professionals to sign up for the latest panacea. Calls come in offering to provide foreclosure lists, lead services, virtual assistants, highly touted algorithm-based software; you name it. All these people want you to pull out your credit or debit card and sign up right now.

You don't need to buy a foreclosure or a tax sale list. Those lists are publicly available online.

Be slow to pull out your card. Do not decide in the moment or buy into anyone's special-deal-if-you-just-buy-now nonsense.

Think about things overnight. Ask your peers what they think of the service or product that you're considering. Protect your money.

43

KEEP YOUR EXPENSES LOW AND GET THEM LOWER.

Keep your business expenses low. Then work on getting them lower. When times are good, people tend to spend big. When times are tight, they wish they had tightened their belts during the good times.

It's easier to save $100 than earn $100. To net $100 in earnings, you must earn about $132 if you are in the 24 percent tax bracket. Yet to keep $100 by limiting your expenses and asking for discounts is simple.

Re-evaluate your subscriptions. Consolidate your debt and lower your interest rates. Increase your insurance deductible if you have the savings to cover a higher deductible. Prepare your meals and eat out less. Check for coupons and rebates. Track pricing history. Join a warehouse club.

If you infrequently use a 40-foot ladder, rent it instead of buying it. Before making a big purchase, sleep on it for one night. Drink more water and fewer sugary drinks. Brew your own coffee. Turn off the lights in unused rooms. Install energy-saving bulbs.

Pay high-interest debt off as quickly as possible. Choose a bank that gives you points, perks, and interest on your money.

One area not to be cheap on is people. Hire the best people and overpay them. Bad hires will cost you a lot of money and time. The best hires will grow your business beyond your expectations.

44

GO TO SEMINARS, YET DON'T SPEND THOUSANDS OF DOLLARS ON MATERIALS IN THE HYPE OF THE MOMENT.

Increasing your real estate education is necessary to build a big business and create a legacy. The education part doesn't have to cost a lot of money. The bulk of the hard-earned money you set aside for real estate investing should go into your properties, not into high-priced seminar materials and elite real estate coaching programs.

You can buy five great real estate investment books for under $100. Read those books. Use your highlighter extensively. Read certain pages or chapters again.

Attend investor seminars and clubs in your area. Some will be more education-based than others. Keep going to the one that provides the most value and skip the ones that don't focus on training or sharing information.

Join some investor groups online. Don't get distracted by the noise of silly or dramatic posts. You are there to learn and contribute.

Many "free" seminars are elaborately designed to sell you a reputed $5,000 product that is reduced just for that day to $995. The people who shell out the $995 are repeatedly pitched to buy the $29,995 elite coaching program.

There is value in paying a reasonable fee for a business coach. Do not pay the whole fee upfront. A great coach will help you turn years into months because you'll use their experience to accelerate your growth. They will hold you accountable to reach the goals that you set.

Be wary of any real estate investment coach who charges a hefty upfront fee to help you find a deal.

45

QUESTIONS ARE THE ANSWER.

"The man who asks a question is a fool for a minute; the man who does not ask is a fool for life." - Confucius

When in doubt, ask questions. When sure of yourself, ask questions.

There are things you know, things you don't know, and things that you don't know that you don't know.

Great questions include:

"Could you tell me more about this, please?"

"This doesn't quite make sense to me. Can you explain why it's being done this way?"

"What is another solution?"

"What is another way that this could work?"

"Can I do something that's in your best interests?"

"What is a question I haven't asked that I should?"

"Who do you recommend that we talk to about this?"

"What are your thoughts on how to solve this?"

Seek advice. Ask for ideas. Come from curiosity, not from judgment. Put the emphasis on the quality of the idea, not on the source of the idea.

46

CONSTANTLY IMPROVE YOUR NEGOTIATION SKILLS.

Negotiation is everywhere. As good as you think you are, you can be better. There are multiple techniques.

Many myths exist about negotiation. Good cop, bad cop is manipulative and backfires most of the time. Making ultimatums ultimately harms you. "Take it or leave it" leaves you in a weaker position most of the time.

Negotiate based on standards, not positions. An example of negotiating on positions is stating, "I know you are asking $250,000 for the house, but I am only willing to pay $200,000." Each side digs into their number or position. An example of negotiating on standards is stating, "A similar home in the neighborhood did indeed sell for $250,000. That home has new windows, stainless steel appliances, new flooring, and a completely remodeled kitchen. In a fair comparison, your house has original windows, older white appliances, worn flooring, and a kitchen that has not been updated. I obtained a contractor estimate for $40,000 for all these improvements. Given that there are usually cost overruns with contractors, the financing costs for me to buy the materials, and the time I personally need to spend to manage the renovation, that is why I'm offering you $200,000. I seek to be reasonable and not pull a number out of thin air."

The first question in any negotiation should be, "Who are they?" Figure out who you are dealing with, from the actual party to anyone who may hold sway with them.

Influence people by influencing the people who influence them. You want to convince the seller to give in to your request? Influence the listing agent they hired. Convince the agent to see your perspective. If they believe that it is in their client's best interests to agree to your request, they may encourage the seller to agree with you.

47

THE PURPOSE OF NEGOTIATION IS FOR THE PARTIES TO BE SATISFIED.

The purpose of a negotiation is not for the parties to be happy. People have different, often convoluted rules about what must happen for them to be happy. The seller of a $500,000 property may only be happy if she receives $700,000, yet no one will pay that much. The buyer of a $500,000 property may only be happy if he can purchase it for $300,000, yet the seller would never even consider that price.

Satisfaction among the parties is the outcome you seek. No one wants to feel manipulated or overpowered in a negotiation. Most of a negotiation is not about the substance of the deal but rather about the people and the process.

A real estate negotiation involves price *and* terms. A seller may agree to a lower price because the buyer agrees to close on the exact date the seller needs. A buyer may agree to a higher price because the seller agrees to leave the riding mower. You cannot know unless you dig a little deeper.

If someone in the negotiation says, "They're not going to be happy with that," instead reply, "What specifically would make them satisfied?"

When the parties are satisfied, you have conducted a successful negotiation.

48

NEVER GIVE A CONCESSION WITHOUT GETTING A CONCESSION.

In a negotiation, if you are asked to give something your automatic response must be, "What are you offering in exchange for that?"

Do not condition yourself to automatically say yes to every request. In negotiation, you give yourself more power when you initially respond with a no than with a yes. If you say yes right away to a request, it is hard to backtrack and say no or ask for something in exchange later. If you say no, then you have the option to say yes later. The other party might even feel like they won a concession from you.

If you are a seller and the buyer asks for a two-week extension, state, "I can consider an extension. What are you offering in exchange for that?"

If you are a buyer and the seller states they wish to take the chandelier in the foyer, state, "I could consider that. What are you offering in exchange for that?"

You will be pleasantly surprised at what you can receive from the other party simply by asking.

49

DON'T PUT TOO MANY WEASEL CLAUSES INTO YOUR CONTRACT.

Weasel clauses are just that—they let you weasel your way out of the contract. Wholesalers love weasel clauses, especially given that many wholesalers cannot actually buy the property they say they may buy.

By all means, consult your legal counsel and your tax adviser to protect yourself. As a buyer, ensure that you perform the level of due diligence that you need. Yet, if you place too many weasel clauses in your offer, you come across as disingenuous.

Sometimes an offer with no contingencies (and no weasels) is what it takes to strike the deal. Make sure the price is something that gives you enough margin for error.

As a cash buyer, typically an inspection or due diligence clause—assuming that you conduct your inspection—is all that you need. If buying with a mortgage loan, add a mortgage contingency clause.

50

MAKE LOTS OF OFFERS AND GO FOR NO.

It is hard to succeed as an investor if your offers are almost always accepted. Make more offers than anyone else you know.

Successful people are told "no" quite frequently. Every no is one step closer to a yes.

If you work with a Realtor, ensure they are well compensated for their time and expertise. Writing a lot of rejected offers does not put food on their family's table.

Make intelligent offers, not lowball offers. An intelligent offer puts equal emphasis on price and terms. It involves finding details from the seller or listing agent about what could work for the seller. Sometimes a seller will take a lower price in exchange for something important to them, such as a specific closing date, having the buyer remove junk, or a waiver of inspections. A lowball offer is simply an offer price well below the asking price without any consideration for terms that the seller may find advantageous.

My wife and I have won several bidding wars for investment properties even though we had the lowest offer price. In each of those multiple-offer scenarios, our offer price was below the asking price. In one situation, the sellers said that they needed to reside in the house for up to two weeks after the closing so they could have a smooth move to their next home. We included a 14-day post-settlement occupancy clause with our offer, and the sellers accepted it. One other note about this negotiation is that when walking through the house, I saw that the husband was a U.S. Navy veteran. I thanked him for his sacrifice, and I told him that I had served in the Navy too. We established a rapport when we briefly talked about our naval experiences. The listing agent later said that the sellers liked me, and that played a role in their decision.

Sometimes the difference between an intelligent offer and a lowball offer can be murky. However, intelligent offers are more likely to be accepted.

51

BECOME MASTERFUL IN NEGOTIATING OVER TERMS AND NOT JUST THE PRICE.

If you go lower on the offer price, make the terms more amenable to the seller. Terms include:

- Closing on the date that is most advantageous for the seller.
- Waiving inspections or agreeing not to negotiate over inspection results.
- Buying in cash or eliminating an appraisal contingency.
- In transactions where an appraisal is necessary, include an appraisal gap contingency to make up some or all of

the shortfall should the appraised value come in lower than the purchase price.
- Allowing the seller to leave debris behind that you will remove at your own expense after settlement.
- Allowing the seller to remain in the property for a short period after the closing date.
- Paying for the seller's closing costs.
- Offering to buy personal property from the seller, such as furniture.
- Paying for the seller's moving costs.
- Offering to pay interest to the seller for years to come in the form of owner financing.
- Convincing the seller and their agent that you will make it a smooth transaction with no unpleasant surprises.

52

SERVE THE UNDERSERVED MARKETS AND MAKE MORE MONEY.

Ever talk to a dog owner who needs to find a rental? Odds are that you'll hear that it's hard to find a landlord who accepts pets. Immigrants who don't speak English well may never even submit a rental application because they don't know how to complete it. A traveling nurse on a 6-month contract prefers a 6-month rental over a hotel room, yet every landlord she finds says they want a 1-year lease. College students want a simple move-in experience in which the landlord provides high-speed Internet, a TV service, and other amenities. Vacationers may complain that there aren't enough furnished short-term rentals near the hottest spots.

As a landlord, you have multiple opportunities to serve certain cohorts who would be willing to pay a premium for the convenience you offer. Study your local market. Look for what's missing or not being served well. If you consider pets for long-term and short-term rentals, you will have no shortage of renters who are happy to pay your price. Flexible lease terms can attract traveling nurses, gig workers, and graduate students.

If there is an acute shortage of housing, building new homes may be lucrative. In some areas, erecting tiny homes profitably may be what the market needs. For higher-end renters, some developers are constructing entire subdivisions with a town square full of shops and restaurants.

The riches are in the niches. Price is only an issue when value is not demonstrated. When you provide value to an underserved market, they will be willing to pay more and stay longer. It'll be a win-win situation.

53

ALWAYS ASK FOR THE BEST PRICE.

"What is the best price you can give me?" If you ask not, you receive not. Asking for a better deal—elegantly—will net you a tremendous amount over a lifetime. You are not being mean, greedy, or ruthless when you simply ask for the best price.

Pause after you ask for the best price. Let the other party respond. You may be pleasantly surprised by what they propose. Perhaps they will lower the price. Perhaps they will keep the price the same yet add something of value. Maybe they will give you a coupon for a future purchase.

You do not pay any taxes when you earn a discount. You don't get what you do not ask for. Be the reason that your dreams have a chance.

54

UNDERSTAND AND EVALUATE RISK.

In any project, consider the worst-case scenario, the best-case scenario, and the most realistic scenario. Think of the things that could go wrong. Are there serious foundation cracks? What if half the tenants don't pay? What if the city issues an order to stop work?

The idea is not to be crippled with worry. The idea is to protect your investment by nipping things in the bud. Stop the monster when it's little, not when it's full-grown and destroying the city.

Every novice house flipper assumes that they will automatically make a profit. That is faulty thinking. You do not make a profit simply because you bought a house and fixed it up. You must know the After Repair Value before making an offer, buy at the right price, manage the renovations well, and sell in a timely manner. Factor in the potential that the house costs more to renovate than planned, sells for less, or takes longer to sell than anticipated.

Many small businesses fail because they are undercapitalized. They simply did not have enough money to continue operations. Evaluate how many months your business can operate on your current savings and income.

How can you reduce your risk?

Negotiate a low enough price that gives you a margin for error.

Conduct a home inspection. You reduce your risk even more when you negotiate a concession because of it (or terminate the deal because it's not worth pursuing).

Obtain a reputable contractor's estimate, preferably before the purchase.

Avoid properties with major structural issues, ongoing water penetration, significant fire damage, or other adverse conditions that will be costly and time-consuming.

Keep sufficient cash reserves for your business *and* your personal expenses.

Work with an experienced Realtor.

Consult your attorney and accountant about asset protection, tax savings, and specific transactions.

Speak with a coach and/or a mentor periodically.

Pay for title insurance.

Check on your property, especially during renovations.

Have proper insurance coverage and enough in savings to cover the deductible.

Perform proper maintenance.

Sign an Operating Agreement if you have business partners.

Have separate accounts for your business and personal expenses.

Change the locks when buying a property and when bringing on a new tenant.

Pull permits and hire licensed professionals.

Connect with the people living right by your property and give them your contact information. They become your eyes and ears.

55

WHEN IN DOUBT, HIRE A PROFESSIONAL.

If you are under contract to buy a property and it appears that the seller is trying to back out of the deal, consult your attorney.

If you have a roof leak, hire a licensed roofer.

If lights are flickering, bring in your electrician.

When selling a property, hire a Realtor or licensed auctioneer.

If your tenant has breached their lease and you're not familiar with how to evict, hire a lawyer who handles evictions.

Their time costs money, but so does your time. The cost of not addressing an issue, or addressing it improperly, is greater than the cost of hiring a professional. When you hire a professional and get it done right, you buy back your time. Maybe you can spend that extra time negotiating your next acquisition.

56

ALWAYS HAVE MORE THAN ONE VENDOR.

Establish relationships with multiple Realtors, mortgage lenders, insurance agents, attorneys, plumbers, electricians, handymen, landscapers, masons, title agents, and so on.

Sometimes your number one choice for plumber is unavailable when you need them. Sometimes your number one choice doesn't service the other side of town. Sometimes your plumber doesn't perform the type of job you need. On larger projects, you should obtain more than one quote.

When vendors know you have options, they won't take you for granted. They will sharpen their pencil to give you the best price. They will fight for your business. You will have more options.

The larger your network, the larger your net worth. You don't know who people know. They might refer you to a motivated seller, a customer, a tenant, a buyer, or a financier. It benefits you to know lots of people.

It's okay to let vendors know that you have more than one business relationship with someone in their field.

57

DON'T ALLOW COGNITIVE SHORTCUTS TO RUIN YOUR DECISION-MAKING ABILITY.

"Once you label me, you negate me."
- Soren Kirkegaard

The human brain develops shortcuts to save time and mental energy, particularly when dealing with threats. If we had to stop and think through every interaction in detail, we could waste time and miss out on opportunities. However, these cognitive shortcuts can cause us to make incorrect assumptions and poor decisions.

Years ago, when I was renovating a house, a real estate investor from the neighborhood invited himself in to see what was happening. He told me how all Realtors are the scum of the earth and then asked me if I was a Realtor. I told him I was and then asked him to leave my house. He instantly lost credibility.

Do not say these things:

"All tenants are…"

"All Realtors are…"

"All contractors are…"

"All wholesalers are…"

"All mortgage brokers are…"

"All buyers are…"

"All people facing foreclosure are…"

"All the people in that neighborhood are…"

"All Section 8 renters are…"

For some people, their highest moment of credibility occurs the split second before they open their mouth. Their credibility nosedives the moment they begin speaking. Think twice, speak once.

58

DO YOUR DUE DILIGENCE OR PAY THE PRICE LATER.

Dealmaking is fun and glamorous. Due diligence is neither. Many investors acquire properties that produce so little value because they become enamored with winning a bidding war or continuing with the momentum of a deal.

There is excitement in making an offer and negotiating the seller down off their initial asking price. The thrill of the chase is palpable. We love to win.

Know the questions to ask. Enlist the help of a Realtor, a home inspector, and a contractor. Consult other professionals as needed. Get a second set of eyes on the property. Take photos or a video so you can share it with someone who cannot make it to the property.

Don't buy real estate just because you feel like buying something. Establish your buying criteria. If a prospective property meets your criteria, make an offer.

If someone is pressing you to make a decision and you are not comfortable, say, "I am not prepared to decide yet. I need additional information to feel comfortable. Can you help me get it?"

59

GET TO THE POTENTIAL DEAL FASTER THAN ANYONE ELSE.

In warfare, it is often much easier to take unoccupied ground and defend it versus having to attack and remove the enemy from occupied ground. Emperor Napoleon Bonaparte used speed as a force multiplier. He trained his men to march farther and faster than the other armies of the day. Napoleon's army could take strategic positions without a fight because they arrived there sooner. In addition, Napoleon's units could maneuver quickly during battle. In the decisive victory over the combined Russo-Austrian army at Austerlitz in 1805, Napoleon's men marched up the Pratzen Heights so quickly that the Russians were soundly defeated when trying to seize that key high ground.

As a real estate investor, find a way to evaluate and see potential deals *before* others do. Look online for deals just before bed or first thing in the morning. Schedule your showings early in the day instead of late in the day. Get there first. Ensure that your advisors—contractor, Realtor, attorney, mortgage broker—know that you like to move quickly and therefore you need them to respond quickly. Be decisive and know your evaluation metrics.

One morning my wife and I saw on the MLS that an end-unit townhouse in a desirable area was just listed for $125,000. We packed up our 1-year-old twins in the car and viewed the house at noon. We submitted a written offer for $122,000 at 2:00 p.m. We stated that we would waive inspections and close in 17 days. We were confident enough to waive inspections since the townhouse appeared to be in good condition and because the Homeowners Association handled exterior maintenance. We chose to use a 15 percent down conventional loan. At 3:00 p.m., the listing agent told us that there were two other offers, both of which were higher than our offer. Around 5:00 p.m. the listing agent told us that the seller had accepted our offer even though it was the lowest price. We spent $1,500 on renovations and rented the townhouse immediately. Less than four years later, that townhouse is worth $238,000 and it produces significant monthly cash flow. Our fixed mortgage interest rate is only 3.375 percent. Had we not moved so quickly, we would have lost out on this fantastic deal.

When your offer is the only one before the seller, you have more bargaining power. If you take two days to evaluate whether to make an offer, in that time other buyers may swoop in ahead of you. Even if the seller wishes to choose you as the buyer, they may negotiate a higher price from you because they have other buyers as options.

If your Realtor or mortgage lender asks you for paperwork, submit it the same day. Move fast.

60

BE WILLING TO WALK AWAY.

In negotiation, you must be willing to walk away from the negotiating table. People can sense when you want something really bad. You must be willing to go without something.

Phrases include:

"With regret, I must decline."

"Unfortunately, this deal does not work for me."

"The numbers don't work here."

"We are just too far apart."

"After careful analysis, I'd be better off not doing this deal."

"Thank you for getting us this far. I really want to make this work with you, yet I'm afraid that I'm asking a little too much from you."

You'll be pleasantly surprised at how many parties bring you back to the table with a better price and terms.

61

"NO" IS A COMPLETE SENTENCE.

A lot of times in life, our troubles originated because we said yes too easily. If you commit to something important by saying yes, you must repeatedly defend that yes by saying no to other things.

When you say no, you do not need to provide a justification or reason. "No" is a complete sentence. "No" can be a no for now. You may need some time to think. You can always say yes later.

It is easier to say yes after you've said no. It is harder to say no after you've said yes. If you are working on something important and someone makes a request of you, your first inclination should be to say no.

The ability to say no will prevent people from taking advantage of you. Your confidence will improve. You will be more productive since you'll create more time for whatever is most important.

62

THE ASKING PRICE IS IRRELEVANT TO AN INVESTOR.

I asked an investor what formula they use to come up with an offer price. They responded, "Whatever the seller is asking, I always offer 30 percent less." That simplistic methodology is deeply flawed. What if the seller's asking price is 50 percent over fair market value? The investor would still pay too much. What if the asking price is 20 percent below fair market value? The investor could offer full price right away and probably snag a hot deal before someone else does.

The seller's asking price is not that important. What matters is the intrinsic value of the property and the opportunity. If the asking price or seller's counteroffer price is too high, a savvy investor simply moves on to the next potential deal.

A wealthy person does not ask, "What will it cost me?" They ask, "What will it make me?"

63

IF A TENANT IS NOT PAYING THEIR RENT, TAKE ACTION.

If a tenant isn't paying their rent, take action. Do not allow weeks to pass. Do not allow your tenant to believe there is no penalty for late payments. Set the tone with your tenant early.

If your tenant has a long track record of paying on time and then is late for the first time, some grace is warranted.

If your tenant is proactive and communicates with you ahead of time to tell you that they will be late, then see what they propose for the solution. If they state that they will pay on the 10th of the month because that is their next payday, give them that opportunity. If they do pay on the 10th as they said, they are a person of their word.

If your tenant does not tell you they will be late with their rent and then waits for you to reach out to them, give them a little grace if they communicate with you on your timing and terms.

Many tenants who are late will hide behind the occasional text message inside of having a phone conversation or face-to-face meeting. If you do not wish to go back and forth via text message over such an important matter as the rent, then tell the tenant that you need to speak with them. Set an appointment to talk. If they ignore you or cancel the appointment, then you need to move forward with the next step.

If dealing with tenants and late rent is too stressful, hire a professional property manager. Even though they are paid a percentage of the gross collected rent, they are worth their weight in gold. A great property manager helps you reduce vacancy and keep operating expenses under control. They also increase your revenue by collecting higher rents, late fees, and revenue from coin-operated laundry machines.

64

INCREASE YOUR RATE OF LEARNING BY MAKING MORE MISTAKES.

Top investors have a history of making mistakes. They take chances, encounter new situations, and fall short many times. Talk to a seasoned investor, and chances are they look back on their biggest mistakes as if those were each a badge of courage.

Most people are afraid of making mistakes. They don't want to look bad. They don't want to appear stupid. They prefer to stay within their comfort zone. Yet new levels of success and fulfillment lie outside of your comfort zone. You typically learn more from your failures than from your successes. If you want to succeed, you must accelerate your rate of failure.

Many people believe that the road to success is one way and the road to failure is in a different direction. However, success and failure are down the same street. Success is just a little farther down the road than failure. In other words, you must go through failure to get to success.

Ask fellow investors, your mentor, and your coach what mistakes they made and what they learned from them. Armed with that knowledge, you don't have to repeat their mistakes. Imagine receiving the value from knowing the lesson without having to pay the price.

Do not allow your confidence to be shaken by missteps. Instead, see every mistake as a valuable learning opportunity. Stack the lessons together to boost your confidence.

A ship at harbor is safe. Yet ships weren't built to stay at the dock. They were designed to go out on the water. You were designed to take on challenges, learn more, and accomplish great things. Take calculated risks. If you are not consistently uncomfortable, you are not growing very much.

Be brave enough to suck at something new.

65

CREATE SYSTEMS.

If you are going to do anything more than once in your business, then you need a system for it. If you wish to build a big enterprise or portfolio of properties, you need to develop and document your systems.

Systems help your employees know what to do, especially in situations where you are not around. Systems create a consistent experience for customers, tenants, vendors, and all others who do business with you.

A successful restaurant has written recipes, the right ingredients on hand, a method for greeting customers and escorting them to their table, a system for preparing the food, and steps for cleaning up.

When you have documented systems, your standards become clear. When people know your standards, they will work to meet them.

THE #1 SKILL FOR SUCCESS IN TODAY'S WORLD IS TO BE INDISTRACTABLE.

Get the best out of technology instead of letting it get the best out of you. Turn off your electronics for one hour a day. Spend that hour thinking, walking in the woods, reading a book, or laughing with your family. Put your phone away when at the dinner table.

Growth-oriented people are curious. However, that curiosity does not have to extend to watching puppy videos at 10:00 a.m. or social media posts at 2:00 a.m. Let your curiosity lead you to learn, not be mildly entertained.

Set up a time block—an appointment with yourself—to focus on a specific task. Naval historian Cyril Northcote Parkinson is noted for Parkinson's Law, which holds that work tends to fill the time allotted for it. Set a deadline for the completion of a task or project. Focus intensely during your time blocks to achieve it.

If a motivated seller asked you to come to their house at 2:00 p.m. to sign a contract to buy it for $150,000 and you knew the house is easily worth $300,000, you would not dare miss that appointment. By the same token, you should not miss an appointment with yourself. However, the world is full of distractions, and it is so easy to ignore your own time block. I know because I've done it myself.

One action I've taken to be accountable is to tell someone close to me that I need their help. I tell them that I'll be focused for the next two hours on completing a specific task. I ask them to check in with me that day so I can report to them how much progress I made.

We all have 24 hours in a day. Yet we see that some people achieve far more than others. A common trait is that successful people set time blocks, typically in the morning, to accomplish important tasks. As the day wears on, their willpower to stay focused will wane. That's okay since they made their mornings highly productive. Keep stacking one productive morning after another.

If you plan to spend 10 minutes a day searching for a hot deal, make those 10 minutes highly effective. Set a timer and tell those near you that you will be focused for the next 10 minutes. Do not allow yourself to look at anything but potential real estate deals. Play music in the background if it helps.

Someone hungrier than you in your area is working hard at this very moment to find the next real estate deal. They're not allowing themselves to be distracted. If you are distracted, they will beat you to the best deals time and time again.

67

THINK FOR ONE HOUR EVERY DAY.

We live in a noisy, distraction-rich world. Thinking is the hardest work, yet it is what leads to breakthroughs. Top CEOs spend time quietly thinking every day. You should too.

Set aside an hour a day to ponder, evaluate, and dream. Write down ideas, no matter how silly. Consider your options. Imagine how to overcome obstacles. Think about delegating, outsourcing, or getting rid of something you don't need to do yourself. Ask intelligent questions.

Your hour of power needs to be scheduled. Don't try to squeeze it in during your commute, your shower, or your workout. This time is an investment in yourself. It is in these consistent appointments with yourself that you will discover multiple action steps that will lead to breakthroughs.

Turn off your phone during your thinking time. Don't check email or social media. Read a book on business or investing.

I graduated business school with Elon Musk. He talks about listening for the signal through all the noise. Take time to separate the signal from the noise. The signal is there. You just need to listen for it during your quiet time.

68

WHEN YOU KNOW WHAT MARKET CYCLE YOU ARE IN, IT'S TIME TO PREPARE FOR THE NEXT MARKET.

There are four basic market cycles: the rising market, the peak market, the declining market, and the trough market. As an investor, you need to know which market you are in, both locally and nationally. Once you know, then you need to prepare for the next market shift.

Follow the real estate and U.S. economic data from the National Association of Realtors at **https://www.nar.realtor/research-and-statistics** or on Twitter by following **@NAR_Research**. Read articles on CNBC at **https://www.cnbc.com/real-estate/**. Check out your local media sources for their real estate articles. Ask your Realtor and fellow investors what market cycle they believe we are in at the moment.

When interest rates go up and banks tighten their lending standards, heavily leveraged investors get squeezed. In market downturns, many house flippers experience financial pressure.

Investors who see the road ahead will make more money in the long run than reactive investors who simply repeat the same behavior.

Are you doing what you're doing today because that's what you did yesterday? Or are you doing what you're doing today because that's the best means of achieving your desired outcome?

69

LOW PRICE DOES NOT ALWAYS MEAN A HIGH PROFIT.

Don't assume that a low-priced property will make you a big profit. A ramshackle house full of unforeseen problems can cost you more money and more time than you planned. A gorgeously renovated home surrounded by poorly maintained houses will not attract top dollar from buyers.

Do not consider a house cheap simply because you are used to higher values in your neighborhood. A person who lives in a $1 million residence in the city should not automatically assume that a $200,000 house in the suburbs is cheap. A potential deal should be evaluated on the comparable sales and renovation costs while considering your exit strategy.

Consider the tangible costs *and* intangible costs of a potential deal. If you plan on doing some work yourself, will that cost you too much in terms of time away from family and friends? If you must learn a new skill like how to tile a bathroom, how much time will it take to finish the job, and what is the cost of the tiles you break along the way? What is the cost of the specialized tools you will need to do a job yourself that a contractor could do instead? If you're renovating on evenings and weekends because you don't want to pay a contractor who will do it faster, what is the extra cost to you in terms of insurance, utilities, and mortgage interest?

A leader does two things:

Solves problems, and

Maximizes resources.

As the leader of your transaction, make your decisions not from the standpoint of always striving for the lowest price but rather from an ethos of maximizing resources.

70

TREAT YOUR FAMILY AS YOUR #1 CLIENT.

When he arrived home one evening, an entrepreneur was on the phone with a disgruntled client who was nitpicking over some inconsequential detail. The entrepreneur's young kids ran over to give him a hug, and he pushed them away so he could focus on the call. Then he realized what he was doing and told the client he was ending the conversation. The entrepreneur swore he would never walk into his home again while on the phone. He would not shoo his kids away.

A mistaken belief among many entrepreneurs is that they must work extremely long hours to build their businesses. They believe that one day in the indeterminate future, they may be so wealthy that they can slow down and finally spend time with their family. That day may not come. And if that day comes, they may have estranged relationships with their family due to their past absences.

Too many entrepreneurs are stuck in day-to-day operations and everyday problems instead of taking time off to think and be with those who matter most. If you're always working, you're probably underleveraged, inefficient, and/or ineffective. You are taking too long to finish your tasks. Some or all of what you're doing could be done by someone else. Perhaps you are doing the wrong things in the first place. A person's wealth is not defined purely by their assets but by their health, lifestyle, and impact with others.

When you walk in the door at home, ensure that you are off the phone when you greet your loved ones. Be present with them. Set boundaries for yourself in your business, and communicate those boundaries to your customers, tenants, contractors, clients, and co-workers. That is what a wealthy person does.

The truth is that you need time to recharge. You need time for exercise and healthy activities. You need to be present for your loved ones now. You can schedule time for yourself, your family, and your friends without compromising the growth of your business.

Look for leverage. Ask yourself, "Who can do this so I don't have to?" Even if you choose not to use leverage in your business now, you can use leverage at home. Hire someone to clean your house, cut your grass, and perform little fixes.

A great businessperson creates time and freedom for themselves and others.

71

BUILD A BOARD OF DIRECTORS FOR YOUR BUSINESS.

No one succeeds alone. When you have an inner circle of trusted advisors, the value they bring is more than you can imagine. If you have a Board of Directors, they will enrich you and won't cost you much. You keep full control of your business, and the profit is all yours. When you have a business partner, you're likely giving up 50 percent of the profits and much of the control.

Who should be on your Board?

- A mentor who is at least two levels above you.
- A peer who is a fellow investor.
- A coach you pay for.
- Your BFF.

If you flip one house a year, a mentor one level above you may be flipping five houses a year. Someone two levels above you may be flipping 25 houses a year. You talk with your mentor on an as-needed basis. Sometimes you may not chat with them for two months, and then you'll talk with them four times over two days. They have been where you have been, and they will have insights to save you time and aggravation.

You should communicate briefly with your peer five days a week. They could be a landlord, flipper, wholesaler, Realtor, or someone else who is a real estate entrepreneur. In the morning, tell them your goals for the day over the phone or via text message. They should likewise share their daily goals. At the end of the day, briefly report to each other how you did. The two of you will push each other to achieve more each day through simple accountability.

Hire a coach. You do not necessarily need to sign a contract and pay monthly or all upfront. It could be a coach who is paid a la carte. A great coach tells you what you need to hear, not necessarily what you want to hear.

Your Best Friend Forever cares for you unconditionally and will tell you the truth, even if it makes you uncomfortable. Share your biggest fears and your loftiest goals with them. If they do not hear from you in a while, they will find you. They will call you out on your BS should you make excuses or pass the blame.

72

DON'T SKIMP ON SAFETY.

Ensure that your properties have smoke detectors and at least one fire extinguisher.

If the fire escape needs work, then do the work.

The number one thing tenants want is to feel safe. If a prospective renter does not feel safe in a home or neighborhood, then they won't stick around to tell you their number two thing.

Put up dusk to dawn or motion sensor lights. Consider an alarm system. Ensure the address numbers are reflective so emergency rescuers can easily spot the home at night.

Fire extinguishers and plungers don't cost much money, but not having them in your rental units can cost you a lot of money. Don't rely on your tenants to buy a fire extinguisher. Provide one for them. It may save a life and your property.

Ensure that all your properties have the proper number and placement of smoke detectors. If a carbon monoxide detector is required, install it. Test them. Even on a fixer-upper you intend to sell, ensure there are enough smoke and carbon monoxide detectors on day 1.

73

SCALE YOUR BUSINESS.

If you can buy one property, you can buy two. If you can buy two, you can buy four. If you can buy four, you can buy eight. The person who owns a thousand units started with one.

Each time you buy a property, you learn new things. You learn which financing is best, who is a great Realtor and who is not suited for investments, and how to evaluate a fixer-upper.

Each time you renovate a property, you learn new tricks of the trade. You learn where to get the discounts, who is a great contractor and who you shouldn't call upon again, and how the city inspectors operate.

Establish systems and write them down. In business, if you are going to do anything more than once you need a system for it.

Here is an example of a Unit Turnover system if you are a landlord:

- When to communicate with the existing tenant about rent increases and the renewal or termination of their lease.
- When and how to advertise the unit will be available.
- When and how to conduct showings with prospective tenants.
- Application and verification process, including storage of applications in process and procedures to shred old applications.
- Checklist for the move-out inspection and procedure to return the security deposit.
- Lease signing procedure and collection of the security deposit and first month's rent.
- Standards and timeframe for the unit to be upgraded in between tenants.
- Access procedures, including lockbox placement and changing of the locks for a new tenant.
- Checklist for the move-in inspection.

It takes different systems and procedures to manage 10 rentals than it does to manage 100. If you are self-managing 10 units, maybe much of what you do is in your head. You should still have important information written down just in case you are incapacitated or away on vacation. I know investors who passed away unexpectedly, and their heirs had no idea what properties were owned, who lived there, or what the lease terms were.

With 100 units, you need written systems that others working with you can easily follow. That ensures that your high standards are upheld consistently.

Other landlord systems include Rent Collection, Maintenance Requests, Property Inspections, Bookkeeping, and Evictions.

Here is an example of a Property Acquisition system if you are a flipper:

- Determine financing options and price range, to include cash, traditional mortgage loan, Home Equity Line of Credit (HELOC), commercial loan, private loan, partnership, credit cards, IRA distribution or loan, and/or hard money.
- Determine if buying in your own name or via an entity.
- Identify target market.
- Determine scope of renovation desired.
- Establish property evaluation criteria, including flipping formula and calculation of After Repair Value.
- Establish exclusive relationship with one Realtor or non-exclusive relationships with more than one Realtor.
- Establish relationships with area investors and wholesalers in case any have a property to sell.
- Prepare and send letters for direct mail campaign.
- Prepare verbiage for text message campaign and transmit messages.
- Place posts and ads on social media.

- Prepare and distribute signage and flyers.
- Research websites of properties for sale, including Zillow.com, Realtor.com, ForSaleByOwner.com, auction.com, hubzu.com, LoopNet.com, and the Multiple Listing Service (MLS).
- Conduct online review of potential properties to determine which ones to see in person.
- Set up showings of ideal property candidates.
- Make offers.
- Once an offer is accepted, conduct property inspection and obtain contractor estimates, if applicable.
- Negotiate, terminate, or proceed with the sale.
- Submit financing application, if applicable.
- Obtain insurance.
- Sign settlement papers.

Other flipper systems include Contractor Selection, Supervision of Renovation, Preparation for Sale, Marketing for Sale, and Bookkeeping.

Every successful business has documented systems that ensure a uniform step-by-step experience and a predictable outcome for each interaction. Professional landlords and flippers use economies of scale to create similar-looking properties. For example, they will use the same paint colors and type of paint across multiple properties.

HOW TO BECOME A WEALTHY REAL ESTATE INVESTOR

How do you quickly close the gap between where you are and where you want to be? Spend time with people who are at the level you wish to be. Do what they do. When you model the best, you turn years into months. Build long-term relationships with wildly successful people.

74

BE PROFICIENT IN THESE FOUR AREAS.

A great entrepreneur is proficient in sales, accounting, leadership, and investing. If you are deficient in any of those areas, the weak area will undermine your business.

Sales is not just being able to sell a house. It is influence. Sales is convincing the right people to work with you. A great salesperson can promote a vision. They know how to convince others to see the possibilities. A great salesperson helps the city inspector make their project a priority. A great salesperson helps a seller decide to pick their offer. A great salesperson influences a contractor to complete the project sooner.

If you don't keep track of your income, expenses, assets, and liabilities, you will pay the price in late fees, back taxes, penalties, and possibly embezzlement. Consult with your accountant. Perform proper bookkeeping or hire someone to do it.

HOW TO BECOME A WEALTHY REAL ESTATE INVESTOR

If you lack leadership skills, you won't attract talented people to your team. You may even attract non-talented people.

The best investors constantly learn. They add new techniques to their repertoire of investing skills. They understand how to calculate the capitalization rate, net operating income, and cash-on-cash return. They recognize that true investment is building a portfolio of appreciating assets over the long term.

75

BE WILLING TO PAY A PREMIUM TO BUY THE HOUSE NEXT DOOR.

Investors naturally wish to purchase their properties at the lowest price possible. There is a saying that when buying an asset, the profit is made on the purchase. Professional landlords and flippers follow proven formulas and criteria to determine their Maximum Allowable Offer (MAO). An investor is safe when they do not offer more than the MAO.

Fishermen talk about "the one that got away." Experienced investors miss out on deals sometimes because of strict adherence to their formulas and criteria. How do you know when to offer more than the MAO? What if your gut says to buy, yet the acquisition price is above the MAO?

You may pay slightly more than the MAO when purchasing a property on the same block, especially the house next door. If you are already pleased with the neighborhood, there are advantages to owning more there.

Regional and national home builders construct many homes in the same subdivision. They enjoy numerous cost savings.

Owning rentals on the same block produces synergies. You have more influence on setting the rents in the neighborhood. It's easier to keep an eye on your properties if they are close to each other. Your contractors won't have to travel far to service your units. Imagine your sense of pride when you own several properties on the same block.

Flippers who turn over properties next to each other already know the neighborhood. They can better predict the After Repair Value and expected days on market. They know what standards to use in renovation. Their contractors are familiar with the area.

When my wife and I bought a townhouse in a desirable subdivision for $122,000, a year later the townhouse directly across the street was listed for $145,000. We looked at it and felt that we should have paid no more than $135,000. We did not buy it. Three years later, that townhouse is worth over $230,000. We should have bought it for $145,000 when we had the chance. It is the one that got away.

How much more should you pay for the house next door? It depends. If you're a landlord, you still need positive monthly cash flow. If you're a flipper, you must still be able to turn a profit. A rule of thumb is up to 15 percent over the MAO.

76

KNOW YOUR BIG WHY.

If you want a big life, you need big money. If you want big money, you need a big business. If you want a big business, you need to take big action. If you want big action, you need a Big Why. Your Big Why is your True North. When times are tough, remember your Big Why to find the strength and resolve to endure.

Your Big Why is a clear vision of what you're looking to achieve. It is the driving force to push you out of mediocrity. Your Big Why includes the people you are working to support. Your Big Why involves you becoming the best possible version of yourself.

When one of my tenants murdered another one of my tenants a few weeks into owning my first investment property, my Big Why helped me move forward. When I had no money left and I was badly in debt, my Big Why kept me going. When people scoffed at me and told me I made stupid decisions, my Big Why helped me keep my head up. When someone initiated a frivolous lawsuit, my Big Why kept me calm. When deals fell apart; when people told me to quit; when I hurt myself doing work on a property; when employees stole; when business partners left; when tenants trashed properties; when contractors disappeared with my money; my Big Why drove me forward through it all.

When I ask people what the purpose of their life is, sometimes the answer I receive sounds like something a person would say on their deathbed: "The purpose of my life, you ask? When I look back on my years, I want to know that I made a difference for hundreds of people. I want people to know that I had no regrets and took risks all the time. I want people to know that I lived a good life…"

Your purpose should be something that you can achieve every single day. You shouldn't have to wait until you're dying to fulfill your purpose.

What is the purpose of my life? *I, Tai DeSa, see, hear, feel, and know that the purpose of my life is to be a leader, investor, and writer, and to do insanely good things for myself, God, and others.* This gives me energy and fulfillment every day.

Setting small goals is not going to move you. Having low motivation will not advance you. Go Big. Take massive action today. Your future self will thank you.

77

BUILD A MOAT AROUND YOUR ASSETS.

Think about asset protection even before you acquire your first property. You worked hard for what you own, and you need to protect it.

The more assets you acquire, the more sophisticated your asset protection systems must become.

Your moat includes property fire/hazard insurance, an umbrella policy, using one or more entities like Limited Liability Companies, legal insurance, trusts, a security system, and preventative maintenance. It includes periodic consultation and reviews with advisors like your attorney, accountant, insurance agent, property manager, and general contractor.

Do not collect cash for rent. If you must do so, let your tenants come to an office and not to your personal residence. Where possible, do not share your home address on paperwork.

Drive carefully to avoid a crash where you are at fault. Do not antagonize situations that could engender a lawsuit against you or your business. The more you grow your wealth, the more of a target you become. Keep a low profile. Don't brag about your wealth on social media.

Create a list of your assets and important contacts, and then give that list to one or two loved ones. If you die suddenly or are incapacitated, your family and heirs should have a clear picture of your portfolio and who to contact. Ensure that your Will is updated periodically.

An investor I knew created just one LLC and put his 20 properties in there. During tough times, he defaulted on multiple mortgage loans, making it difficult to segregate his assets. His bad apples poisoned the whole bunch. The idea of creating an LLC is to limit the number of properties in there. A rule of thumb is one to three properties per LLC.

Every situation is different, so consult your advisors about asset protection.

78

MAKE ONE MORE CALL.

The difference between a massively successful investor and a mediocre performer is not a chasm but a matter of inches. A top performer practices more. They do a little more. They are consistent in those small efforts, which add up to a lifetime of advantages.

If you are evaluating a potential renter, make one more call to be sure they are the right fit. If you are calling potential sellers, make one more call before you go on to the next thing. If you are researching a property, make one more call as part of your due diligence. If you are trying to find the right mortgage lender, make one more call to consider another option.

Anyone can do anything for 15 seconds. Stack 15 seconds of additional activity back-to-back. Keep doing a little more, day after day.

79

KEEP A JOURNAL.

If life is worth living, then it is worth recording. Keep a written journal. Jot down your dreams, your goals, and your magic moments. Keep a section for great questions. Great questions make you think. Questions are the answer.

Record your mistakes with pride. Every great entrepreneur has screwed up multiple times. When you write down your mistakes, include what caused them. Was it pride, arrogance, impulsiveness, or analysis paralysis? When you record your mistakes and see them as an accelerant for success, you are highly unlikely to repeat them.

80

OWN WHAT YOU CAN RENT TO OTHERS ONE DAY.

When you purchase a home for yourself, choose something that would make a great rental. Enjoy living there. Should you move out one day, keep the property and rent it out either as a long-term or vacation rental. Many investors build a collection of rentals that were their former homes.

My first home was a fixer-upper duplex. I lived in one unit while renovating it. When it was complete, I rented it and lived in the other unit while fixing it. Then I rented the second unit. Even though I only lived there for three years, I kept the property for 17 years. I only sold it via a 1031 tax-deferred exchange after I moved to another state.

Don't buy a home that you know you won't be able to rent for a profit in the future. If you purchase a luxurious residence with a fantastic view, consider turning it into a short-term rental if the property won't produce positive cash flow as a long-term rental. If short-term rentals may be the better option one day, ensure that the area you live in allows them.

Many great investors build a collection of former residences over the years.

81

GIVE, WITH PURPOSE.

To whom much is given, much is expected. Even when you have little, give to the less fortunate. You don't have to give money until it hurts; give until it feels good. Give your time. Volunteer. Mentor. Coach. Buy the box of Girl Scout cookies from the kid at the entrance of the supermarket.

Give with no expectation of return. Tithe. Smile broadly when giving. Your heart will sing. Make giving a part of your Big Why.

82

PEOPLE SHOW YOU WHO THEY ARE. BELIEVE THEM.

The contractor who only returns one of five phone calls you make to him is telling you that you're not a priority. Believe him, and don't hire him again.

The business partner who promises you they will do one thing and then does the opposite is telling you that your input doesn't matter. Believe her and consider ending the partnership.

The tenant who ignores your phone calls when they are late on the rent yet badgers you when they have a repair request is telling you that they are not about a win-win relationship. Believe him and do not renew their lease.

The lawyer who tells you that they will work on your contract yet ignores your requests for an update is telling you that they prefer to spend time on other clients. Believe her and find an attorney who values your business.

People show you who they are. You just need to believe them.

83

ONE DOLLAR OF PASSIVE INCOME IS WORTH 10 DOLLARS OF ACTIVE INCOME.

Most people focus on maximizing their active income, the money they earn from working. Most wealthy people focus on maximizing their passive income, which is the money they earn from sources that require little to no work. Most people have zero passive income streams. Nada. Zilch. Nothing.

Passive income starts small. It grows slowly at first. It gets dwarfed by the amount of active income.

If you asked me whether I would rather earn $50,000 in a year from flipping a house or earn $5,000 in a year in cash flow from owning a rental house, I would rather keep the house and earn the $5,000 per year.

Active income is taxed more heavily than passive income. Passive income grows even when you're not involved. You make money while you sleep.

Put a lot of attention into earning every additional dollar of passive income that you can. Add more every year.

84

INVEST EVERY DOLLAR OF PASSIVE INCOME INTO ANOTHER ASSET THAT PRODUCES PASSIVE INCOME.

If you receive cash flow from a rental, save that passive income so it can be the down payment for another rental. Track every dollar of passive income. Set it aside in a high-yield savings account for new opportunities. You want that savings account to be flexible so you can pull the money out quickly without penalty.

If you make $800 a month in cash flow from your first rental unit, do not spend it on personal expenses. Put that money in the high yield savings account. Add more money to the account from your day job. Use the money for a down payment on your next rental property. Then invest the cash flow from both properties into the savings account while you search for the next deal.

HOW TO BECOME A WEALTHY REAL ESTATE INVESTOR

If you are a flipper, put your sale proceeds into the savings account. Estimate your capital gains taxes. The money for taxes will stay in your savings account until tax time. If your sale proceeds are $50,000 and your estimated taxes are $10,000, you will only pull out $40,000 for the next deal. You will never fall behind on taxes, and your tax money will earn interest before you give it to Uncle Sam.

In a few years, your passive income will grow dramatically. One day you'll be able to live entirely off your passive income and still have more to give away and invest.

Financial freedom is having your passive income streams exceed your lifestyle expenses.

Many people believe wealth is directly related to their income. However, many high-income earners couldn't last more than a few months if their active income suddenly stopped.

Use your active income to acquire assets that produce passive income. Then combine that passive income with your active income to acquire more assets that produce passive income. Repeat.

85

CREATE MULTIPLE INCOME STREAMS.

Every year, find a way to add at least one new income stream. That includes side hustles and passive income. Income streams include acquiring more rental units, coaching fees, book royalties, content creation fees, setting up a coin-operated laundry room in your rental building, referral fees, owning dividend-paying stock, interest on loans, commissions, a new business, and returns from investments in syndicates.

The typical self-made millionaire has a primary source of income and at least five additional income streams.

When I was in the Navy, to supplement my current income I purchased dividend-paying stocks and worked as a private tutor for some high school students. After leaving the Navy, I bought commercial and residential rental properties. I created a couple of networking groups that generated income when the members paid annual dues. I signed up for a handful of multi-level marketing businesses through the years, most notably a company that provides legal insurance. I issued some short-term loans to investors. I obtained my real estate broker license and earned commission on sales. I became eligible for profit-sharing from the real estate brokerage I joined. I created a weekend investment seminar and asked some nationally recognized experts to fly in and sell their educational products.

After marrying, my wife and I bought shares in a local title company and a local insurance company. We acquired more rentals. I self-published some books and received royalties. I served as the CEO of a real estate brokerage. We organized some investment seminars and charged admission. I created a coaching business for entrepreneurs and real estate investors. We applied for and received some business grants. We set aside money in a high-yield savings account. All these income streams give us joy and freedom. We live a life by design.

Add at least one new income stream every year. Ensure that most new income streams are passive ones, so you are not trading in more of your time for money.

86

ENSURE THAT YOU HAVE SIGNED LEASES.

No tenant should ever take possession of your property without a fully signed lease. To not have a signed written lease in place is mismanagement.

You devalue your property when you do not have a signed lease. If you are attempting to sell the property, most buyers will feel less secure about the situation and therefore offer less. Some would-be buyers will not even make an offer because their lender will require written leases as a condition of the loan. If you are obtaining an appraisal, the appraiser may adjust downward for the lack of a long-term lease. If you're seeking to refinance the property, the bank underwriter might not give you credit for the income. Some banks will not even grant a refinance to you without a signed long-term lease in place. Multi-year leases on commercial rentals increase the value dramatically.

Without a lease, you increase the risk of conflict between you and the tenant due to misunderstandings of what is allowed. Tenants may sublet to people you did not approve since you failed to state in a lease that subletters are not permitted or that subletters require landlord approval. Extreme behavior by a tenant, or their guest or customer, will be harder to enforce since such behavior was not expressly prohibited in a lease.

A written lease creates the rules for a business relationship. A written lease protects the tenant and the landlord.

If you do not have a written lease, it's easy to get one. Talk to your attorney or Realtor.

87

DON'T CANNIBALIZE ONE UNIT TO FIX ANOTHER UNIT.

If one of your properties needs a new faucet, do not replace it with a used faucet from one of your vacant units. If one of your houses needs a stove, do not pull the existing stove out of one of your other projects. Cannibalizing your units for parts and equipment does not save you money. It wastes your time. Running from property to property and trying to remember which piece is where is folly.

Each unit or project should be able to support itself. Enough money should be set aside for each project. When a dwelling needs a part, an appliance, or some other fix, acquire the materials needed from a store.

88

NEVER GO MORE THAN THREE STRAIGHT YEARS WITHOUT INCREASING THE RENT.

An amateur landlord keeps the rent the same year after year. Years ago, I met a landlord who owned a 2-bedroom unit like me. I said that I believed the market rent for 2-bedrooms was $750 a month, which I was receiving for my unit. He replied that he had been charging his tenant $250 a month for the past 20 years. I stated that his rent was too low and asked why he never raised it. He replied that he felt bad asking for more and feared having the unit be vacant.

Reasons to increase the rent:

- To keep up with inflation.

- Build up a reserve for anticipated capital expenditures (the unit needs a new roof after 30 years) and unanticipated capital expenditures (the roof leaks after a major storm and needs to be fixed or replaced). If you fail to build up a reserve, you harm yourself and your tenant.
- Increase the value of the property. Rental properties, especially multi-unit residential and commercial properties, are typically valued using the income approach. The more income for a stabilized multi-unit, the more a bank would be willing to lend and the more a buyer would be willing to pay.
- Increase profit. The purpose of business is to fund the perfect life. The measure of business is profit.

Cost only becomes an issue when value is not demonstrated. If you want more rent, offer more value.

In economic downturns, it makes sense to keep rent the same or lower it slightly to avoid high vacancy. Economic downturns come and go. When you raise the rent periodically, your tenants expect it.

Let your tenants know 6 to 12 months in advance what the rent will be when the lease renews. That helps them budget for it. It also helps them psychologically accept it. When utility providers increase their rates, they inform customers 12 consecutive months in advance. When the time comes for the rate increase, the customers accept it because they've been told about it over and over.

89
GIVE YOUR SPOUSE OR BUSINESS PARTNER VETO POWER.

If you are married or have a business partner, give them veto power on any property purchase. In other words, you cannot purchase a property unless all partners agree that you should.

You should present why you recommend buying a property for a specific price and terms. If they say no after fully listening to the reasoning, then do not buy the property. Look for something else. Perhaps their evaluation reveals a risk that is not worth taking. Besides, there is no need to create conflict or an "I told you so" moment by moving forward with a real estate purchase against the wishes of your partner. There are plenty of other deals out there to find and consider.

Many years ago, I created a company with a couple of business partners. The rule was that we would only buy a property if all three partners agreed. One day, without my knowledge, on a whim they took company money and bid on parcels at a county tax sale. They had done absolutely no research. They saw a man in the front row bidding on some lots, and they thought he seemed to know what he was doing. So, they decided to bid on whatever parcels he was trying to buy. My two partners bought several junk lots that day. It took us months to sell the land. We eventually broke even after a lot of time and energy was spent on selling the parcels.

Great things will happen when you are fully aligned with your spouse or business partner. They will appreciate that you value their opinion and that you value their money.

90

IF YOUR SPOUSE OR PARTNER IS COMPLETELY AGAINST OWNING INVESTMENT REAL ESTATE, INVEST IN REITS.

Owning real property and following certain principles increases your wealth over time. However, your spouse or partner may not see the opportunities that you see. They may evaluate risk differently. They may believe that a different asset class is superior. They may feel that now is not the time to invest.

First, discern the position of your spouse or partner regarding owning real estate:

Is it a permanent no?

Is it a yes, but a no for now?

Is it a yes, but a no for this particular property?

There are ways to profit from real estate without owning the real estate. You can be a wholesaler. You can be a private money lender. You can obtain your real estate license and broker deals for others.

If you wish to own real estate yet your partner is concerned about risk or believes the timing is not right, buy shares in a Real Estate Investment Trust (REIT). You will have no management responsibility and no legal liability. You can receive dividends. In many REITs, your investment is liquid, meaning you can sell your shares easily.

U.S. News & World Report has a list of REITs to consider at **https://money.usnews.com/investing/slideshows/best-reits-to-buy**. Jim Cramer of CNBC's Mad Money gives periodic REIT recommendations. Vanguard has a real estate index fund with ticker symbol VGSIX.

You do not need to own an investment property to receive some of the benefits of investment in real estate.

91

ADD SOMETHING NEW EVERY YEAR.

If you aren't growing, you're dying. Stagnation is not an option.

Add something new and challenging every year. Buy a rental house in the nostalgic neighborhood that reminds you of your youth. Enjoy furnishing one of your units and make it a short-term rental. Acquire a mixed-use property. Obtain your real estate license. Establish an office. Hire an assistant. Start an investing club that meets the first Wednesday of every month. Write a book. Build a following on social media. Create how-to videos. Mentor a new investor. Help build a home through Habitat for Humanity.

Demonstrate your capacity for growth. Big responsibilities go to the people who prove their ability to handle small responsibilities. You'll become more confident, well-rounded, and better able to develop new solutions to challenging problems.

92

LOWEST PRICE DOES NOT EQUAL LOWEST COST.

Many believe that the more money they save, the more they will make. A past business partner of mine insisted upon hiring the cheapest possible contractor to handle the renovation of a house that we were planning to flip. My partner believed the key to maximizing profit is finding the person who will charge the least for a job and then negotiating them even lower. After the sole proprietor gave his estimate, the partner told him to cut his price even more, lest we go with someone else. Desperate for work, the contractor did so.

The contractor completely missed the deadline for completion. He failed to finish the job. He purchased substandard materials to save money and attempted to install discarded materials from another project. The contractor cut corners. The contractor focused his energy on other customers who were paying more, so our project was only handled occasionally. Eventually, he stopped responding to us, and we knew that we had to bring someone else in to do the job. The work that the first contractor performed had to be undone by the second contractor, which cost us even more money.

Lowest price does not equal lowest cost. Lowest price does not mean biggest profit. Just because someone gave the lowest bid does not mean you will minimize your costs and maximize your profit. When you obtain estimates from contractors, your objective is not to automatically hire the one with the lowest quote. Your outcome is to pick the contractor who will provide the most value. Value includes the time it takes to do the job, the skills to do it to your standards, having insurance and licenses that are current, the form of payment accepted, communication skills, and integrity. If they don't have integrity, the other things don't matter.

Beware of a contractor whose estimate is far below the other estimate(s) you obtain. Some contractors bid extremely low to convince you to hire them since they desperately need the money to finish another job. They collect a hefty deposit upfront and might even perform a little work before ghosting you. Lowest price does not mean lowest cost. After weeks of chasing a ghost, you will have to hire a new contractor.

If you find a contractor who under-promises and over-delivers, keep working with them. Ditto if the contractor stands by their work should a problem occur after the job was completed.

93

PUT YOUR FOCUS MORE ON BEING EFFECTIVE THAN ON BEING EFFICIENT.

Being efficient at painting rooms means that you're getting faster at painting. Yet that efficiency only marginally increases your profitability as a real estate investor.

Being effective is finding and negotiating more deals. Sure, you could save $2,000 by painting a house yourself. Or, in the time it takes to do that, you can discover another deal that adds $50,000 to the bottom line.

Being efficient is doing things right. Being effective is doing the right things.

Constantly look to do the right things that grow your business and increase your opportunities.

94

HAVE AT LEAST SIX MONTHS OF WORKING CAPITAL.

Many people are only two to three months away from financial ruin if they lose their job. Many businesses could not last more than a few weeks if their main source of income suddenly stopped.

What if your main source of income dried up overnight? How would your business fund its operations? Businesses can fail because of undercapitalization.

Keep and build up an emergency reserve for your business. Keep it in an interest-bearing account if possible. Having at least six months of money set aside helps you weather economic downturns. If you spot a lucrative opportunity, you can act on it.

In your lifetime, every asset class, including residential real estate and commercial real estate, will experience a drop in value of 40 percent or more. These downturns are almost always unanticipated. Your reserve fund will come in handy during tumultuous times, both as a lifeline for your business and as capital to buy assets that are on sale.

95

THE THREE QUESTIONS TO ASK WHEN HIRING SOMEONE.

Can they do the job? Will they do the job? Is it a good team fit?

In business, you are typically one or two great hires away from freedom. The right hire will propel your business and allow you to have more time for other things. The wrong hire can disrupt your business, costing you time and money.

The toughest choice for many new entrepreneurs is when to make their first hire. Many entrepreneurs fear losing control. They say that if you want it done right, you have to do it yourself. So, they put off hiring others. The truth is that the right person will do the jobs you give them better than you can.

If you question a potential hire's integrity, then don't bother trying to answer the other questions. Find someone better.

Take your time choosing a new hire. Don't hire someone quickly just because you feel overwhelmed. Many entrepreneurs only hire someone when they are overloaded with tasks. You want to build the factory before you receive the orders for widgets. Plan for the work needed and hire in advance.

Ensure that you have a training program in place. Your new hires should receive quality training the minute they start their first shift.

When you hire someone new, have a formal meeting on the 30th day, the 60th day, and the 90th day on the job. Each of those three meetings is to evaluate their work to see if they are a match to continue working. After 90 days, both of you should know if they are a good match. If they are not a good match, they should know it is time to pursue a different opportunity.

To attract top talent, you must be the type of person that top talent wants to work for. Ask yourself, "Who do I need to be to attract and retain the type of talent who will grow my business beyond my wildest dreams?"

Top entrepreneurs are in a constant state of searching for talent to join their teams. Sometimes the right person comes along when you don't have any positions open. For top talent, you should create a position.

In your business, you should not be the only innovator. You want a company that innovates.

96

IN THE LONG RUN, THE CONSTRAINT ON YOUR BUSINESS IS YOUR AMBITION.

A person with great ambition can face tremendous setbacks in the short-term such as a market downturn, unanticipated costly repairs, a lawsuit, the death or sickness of a loved one, a tough Zoning Board, or insufficient financing. However, in the long term, a business led by an ambitious person will grow despite the inevitable challenges of life.

A person with little ambition can receive great success in the short-term such as a rapidly rising market, easy access to capital, an easygoing Zoning Board, or an inheritance deployed into the right assets at the right time. However, in the long term, the business is constrained by the owner's ambition.

Why does one real estate investor own three properties and another owns 300 properties? In the short-term, it could be any of a number of reasons. Over a period of decades, it comes down to the ambition of the investor. An ambitious entrepreneur finds a way to grow the business despite setbacks.

Do not let a lack of ambition constrain your investment portfolio. Keep growing it.

97
FIND WAYS TO MAKE REAL ESTATE INVESTING FUN.

Find ways to make real estate investing fun. See the hidden opportunity in every situation. Enjoy learning about carpentry, architecture, kitchen cabinetry, or landscaping. Smile with your contractors, tenants, and advisors. Enter the room with energy. Leave people feeling good.

Play music when analyzing a deal or working on a property. Bring someone to your latest fixer-upper and ask their opinion on the kitchen remodel. Personally thank every contractor and subcontractor working on your property.

Mentor someone who wants to get into investing. If you complete your objectives for the week, reward yourself by seeing a matinee on Friday.

Tell a funny story about how you made a colossal mistake in investing. Every self-made person has a collection of stories about how they screwed up. Making mistakes is the badge of courage of wealthy people. Share those stories with pride.

98

FIX THE PROBLEM, NOT THE BLAME.

"In any situation, the person who can most accurately describe reality without laying blame will emerge as the leader, whether designated or not." - Edwin Friedman

Don't let setbacks send you into a downward spiral. If you encounter an obstacle, it's okay to feel frustrated for a moment. Then, get to work. Fix the problem, not the blame. Involve your team in the solution.

People assume that blame accomplishes two things: 1) It assigns responsibility, and 2) It solves problems. However, blame does neither well. Blame causes others to avoid you, deflect, go silent, or fight back. People who are being blamed are less likely to be creative or motivated to work with you.

Therefore, all blame is useless. Blame does not provide an optimal solution to the problem before you. Choose a more empowering approach.

Be less interested in how we got here. Be more interested in where we are going. Spend more time talking about the solution.

When you behave in a blameless, empowering manner, you truly empower others to be part of the creative solution. You will come across as a leader.

99

FOCUS ON GETTING RICH FOR SURE INSTEAD OF GETTING RICH QUICK.

There is a whole cottage industry on how to get rich quick through real estate. Two decades ago, I spent thousands of dollars on gurus, seminars, and courses. Armed with that knowledge, I did lease purchases, lease purchase wraps, installment contracts, pre-foreclosures, foreclosure auctions, wholesaling, flipping, single-family rentals, multi-family rentals, mixed-use rentals, commercial rentals, short sales, buying straight from the bank, and subject-to transactions. I bought with my money, private money, hard money, seller financing, and traditional mortgage financing. I bought on my own; I bought in my own name; I bought with partners; I created joint ventures; I created LLCs, LPs, and C Corps.

I self-managed my rentals; I hired employees to manage my rentals; I hired property management firms; I created my property management firm. I worked without Realtors; I worked with Realtors; I became a Realtor; I created a couple of brokerages; I joined a national brokerage; I expanded to another state. I bought short sales; I negotiated short sales in multiple states; I sold short sales. I worked from home; I leased Class A office space. I bought and sold in up markets and in down markets. I was as creative with real estate as anyone could be.

I became experienced through creative real estate but did not become rich through creative real estate. I became wealthy over time through owning rental properties in working-class neighborhoods. It is slow, unexciting, involves saving money, and is hard work at times, yet it is a sure path to wealth. Positive monthly cash flow, using the rent to pay down a mortgage loan, letting depreciation work for you, and having properties appreciate in value create the slow and steady path to financial freedom. The best way to become wealthy fast is to become wealthy with a sure thing over time.

In the military, we would say, "Slow is smooth, and smooth is fast."

You don't need to master multiple creative real estate techniques. You don't need a glitzy commercial office. You don't need to do hundreds of deals. You just need something slow and boring to get rich.

100

BUILD WEALTH THAT WILL OUTLAST YOU.

In a culture of fast food, same-day or next-day deliveries, buy-now-pay-later options, and instantly available information, many people only think of the short-term. Even at major companies, many CEOs think only of the current quarter and not the next 5, 10, or 50 years. After all, many of their shareholders only expect the stock price to go up right away.

There is nothing wrong with living in the here and now. Cherish magic moments and spend time with those who matter most. However, do not operate exclusively for the short-term and ignore the long-term.

You can build generational wealth with well-selected and well-managed real estate. The federal tax code encourages investors—through provisions like depreciation, 1031 tax-deferred exchanges, trusts, and a stepped-up tax basis for your heirs—to hold and rent real estate for many years.

You owe it to yourself and the generations who follow to educate yourself, plan your estate, and build your portfolio. Even if you do not have heirs or desire to have children, there is a powerful potential impact that your wealth can have on your community for decades to come, even long after you're gone.

101

BE A VICTOR, NOT A VICTIM.

Things don't happen to you. They happen for you. A successful investor will have setbacks. Either you win, or you learn. Sometimes the lessons you learn, however painful, are exactly what you need.

Be brave enough to suck at something new. Take that chance. Fail forward.

When things don't go their way, a person with victim mentality places blame on others. That mentality protects a person in the moment, yet it cripples them for life. When someone plays the role of a victim, they are saying that they don't have to change. Their blame on others is basically saying that for things to be different, other people need to change. It feels comforting in the moment, yet it never forces the person to examine themselves and inspire themselves to grow.

A victim believes that they didn't get what they want because of a lack of resources. Yet the truth is that when we fail, it is because of a lack of resourcefulness. We didn't use all that we had at our disposal.

Instead of being a victim, choose to be the victor. When things don't go your way, take responsibility for the results. It is empowering. Change course. Take on a new perspective. Bring in new resources. Be more resourceful. Be more passionate. Take full responsibility for your own growth and results. By doing so, you will achieve far more than you thought possible.

EPILOGUE

Thank you for reading this book. Keep referring to specific or random pages as you sharpen your real estate investing skills. Step out of your comfort zone. Play the long game. Do what is right. When you invest in real estate, perhaps the greatest benefit is that you will transform into the best possible version of yourself.

This book is part of the Invest & Transform educational resources for investors.

To go into more detail on a variety of real estate topics, go to my website at **https://investandtransform.com/**

Like my Facebook Page for investors at **https://www.facebook.com/investandtransform**

Follow me on Instagram as I share investing tidbits at **https://www.instagram.com/desatai/**

Subscribe to my YouTube channel at **https://www.youtube.com/@investandtransform1127**

Connect with me on LinkedIn at **https://www.linkedin.com/in/taidesa/**

Send me an email at **tai@investandtransform.com** to let me know how your wealth-building journey is going!

ABOUT THE AUTHOR

Tai A. DeSa grew up in Stroudsburg, Pennsylvania, as the oldest of 11 children. He was the valedictorian of the Class of 1993 at Notre Dame High School in East Stroudsburg. He graduated from the Wharton School at the University of Pennsylvania in 1997.

DeSa then joined the U.S. Navy. He completed Officer Candidate School and was commissioned as an officer in January 1998. He completed multiple overseas deployments, participating in Operation Joint Guardian, Operation Enduring Freedom, and Operation Iraqi Freedom.

DeSa left the Navy to become a full-time real estate investor in 2004. Four years later, he obtained his real estate license in Pennsylvania. In 2015, DeSa took a role leading a Keller Williams Real Estate office to be the #1 brokerage in its market. DeSa is now a real estate broker in Pennsylvania and Tennessee. He coaches and consults real estate investors and entrepreneurs.

DeSa loves working in real estate with his wife, Amira. They own multiple rental properties. They are thrilled to be raising their twin daughters, Alexis and Ashley. DeSa wants you to lead a life by design, not by default.

ACKNOWLEDGMENTS

I would like to first and foremost thank my beautiful wife, Amira. I am grateful for my twin daughters Alexis and Ashley. And of course, thank you to my parents who influenced me to be the person I am today. Thank you to my siblings Sa, Truc, Tri, Van, Tam, Trinh, Thanh, Trung, Hong, and Thang. Thank you to Amira's parents, Al and Helen Harb, for keeping an eye on Alexis and Ashley when I needed time to write.

To my son, Creed Daniel DeSa, who is with Jesus in Heaven.

The Charity of Choice for me is KW Cares. Go to **https://www.kwcares.org/** for more information.

Made in the USA
Columbia, SC
19 September 2024